EVERY WOMAN HAS A STORY

A Collection of Short Stories

LAUREL KILE

Copyright © 2023 Laurel Kile
Laurel Kile
Every Woman Has a Story
A Collection of Short Stories
All rights reserved.

No part of this publication may be reproduced, distributed, or transmitted in any form or by any means, including photocopying, recording, or other electronic or mechanical methods, without the prior written permission of the author, except in the case of brief quotations embodied in critical reviews and certain other non-commercial uses permitted by copyright law.

Printed in the United States of America
First Printing 2023
First Edition 2023

Ebook- 979-8-9893019-0-4
Paperback- 979-8-9893019-1-1

DEDICATION

To my husband, thank you for your support and patience.

To my daughters, Alexandra and Lillian. I love you to the moon and back.

To my mom, aunts, sisters, mentors, teachers, and friends, thank you. Strong women build up strong women.

"Here's to strong women. May we know them. May we be them. May we raise them."
– Unknown

"Raise your glass if you are wrong in all the right ways."
–Pink

"Wrinkles only go where the smiles have been."
–Jimmy Buffett

Table of Contents

The Breaking Zone 1

Driving East with My Daughters....................................... 45

Auntie P, The Matchmaker 84

Quarantined with a Stranger 128

An Afternoon with Clara 171

About the Author 193

Random Thoughts from the Author................................. 195

Acknowledgements... 197

Other Titles by the Author 198

1

The Breaking Zone

Morning is my favorite time to come to the beach. There's no splashing children or drunk, sunburned tourists pushing each other into the water. It's just me, shell-seekers, and the peaceful waves.

Well, most days, they were peaceful. Last night, thunderstorms slammed the Atlantic coast, turning the gentle surf into boisterous whitecaps. Lifeguards on four-wheelers sped up and down the shoreline, hoisting double red flags, announcing that the beach was closed for swimming.

I looked at my watch and sighed. It was almost 7:30. I only had a few more minutes to myself before my parents or sister would come looking for me. That morning, I'd intentionally slipped out the door before anyone was awake and left my cell phone on the kitchen island. My mother would probably be worried, but I just couldn't bring myself to care.

Don't get me wrong, I loved my mom. In fact, I had an amazing family. But this particular morning, I needed my space. It was my wedding day.

Well, it was supposed to be my wedding day.

Three weeks ago, Trevor, my college sweetheart, called off the wedding — with absolutely no warning.

Since then, I'd spent every waking minute wracking my brain, trying to think of what more I could have done to make him happy. During our junior year, when he decided to go to law school, I pushed myself to the breaking point, taking twenty-one-hour semesters so that I could graduate early and bring home a paycheck. When he decided that law school wasn't his dream, I moved to Nashville so he could intern for a record label. When he joined a megachurch that demanded we stop living in sin, I moved into a studio apartment until after the wedding.

Whatever dream he had, I supported him with my whole heart. So, when he called to say I wasn't the woman he saw himself growing old with, I was blindsided and humiliated.

My family, however, wasn't exactly devastated. Since the ending of our engagement, they had shared some concerns about Trevor. Well, concerns may be putting it mildly; all out loathing seems more appropriate.

I'd always believed my parents and sister thought of Trevor as a member of the family. Turned out, they considered him the loud, drunk uncle that everybody hoped would forget to show up on Thanksgiving.

My father had been the most reserved in his assessment. "Simone, if I thought he made you happy, I'd tell you to chase that boy down and fight for him. But I never remember you smiling when he was around."

My mother said, "I never liked that boy. He reminded me of a weasel, always 'getting ready' to do something big, but never actually doing it."

"He never cared about your dreams," my sister, Naomi, told me over margaritas. "Did he ever once ask if you wanted to move to Nashville or how you felt about that megachurch where you spent all your free time? If you ask me, you dodged a bullet."

My grandmother was the least eloquent. "If that boy were on fire, I wouldn't lift my leg to piss on him."

One would think that all these opinions about how selfish Trevor was or how I'd dodged a bullet would make me happy or, at least, relieved. Instead, it made me feel stupid. Why didn't I see what was crystal clear to so many others? And now that I did see, why did I still long for him? What kind of pathetic loser pines away for such a poor excuse of a partner?

My watch vibrated. It was a text from Mom: **Simone, where are you?**

I pinched the bridge of my nose. "So, now I need to leave my watch behind as well." I muttered as I pushed myself to my feet and started back toward the house. As I got further away from the water, the ground under my feet evolved from sugar-fine sand to jagged pieces of seashells, where last night's storm had deposited debris from the ocean floor onto the beach. It lay in a tidy line that paralleled the shoreline. As a kid, I'd called that section of beach the breaking zone.

I picked up a shell fragment, turning it over and over in my hand. I could tell it had once been a part of a conch, rough and tan on one side while milky white on the other. I wondered what the shell looked like when it was whole. It had probably been quite beautiful. I'd once felt beautiful, but now, just like the shell, I was battered, tossed around, and irreversibly broken.

I took my time climbing the wooden stairs that led to the rooftop deck of our beach house. Thankfully, Dad was the only one on the deck when I arrived. He was reading the local newspaper as I plopped myself into the Adirondack chair beside him. "Why are you reading that? You don't know any of the people or places that are mentioned in those stories."

He folded the paper and sat it on his knee. "Doesn't mean they aren't stories worth reading. Did you know that a junior from First Flight High School just signed to play golf at The University of Ohio? They think he could be the next Bubba Watson."

"I learned something new today." I sat back in the chair and closed my eyes. "Is First Flight the school in Kitty Hawk?"

"Right down the road in Kill Devil Hills. Speaking of which, we saw that the beach is closed this morning. Naomi and Chris were thinking of taking the boys to the Wright Brothers Monument today. Remember how you used to love that place when you were a girl?"

I nodded. "It's a beautiful monument."

"It was a masterful feat in engineering, too. Twelve hundred tons of granite atop a mountain of sand." He whistled through his teeth. "Did you know that they used lumber from Cass to build their first plane?"

I couldn't help but smile. Dad was a born and bred West Virginian. He got his engineering degree from West Virginia University and had grown up in Marlinton, WV, just down the road from the Cass lumber camp. In the early 1900s, Cass had been one of the main providers of lumber for the eastern United States, including the bike shop of Orville and Wilber Wright. Dad took every chance he could to tell people that the first airplane was made with lumber from his own backyard.

I nudged Dad with my elbow. "It's a fact you may have mentioned once or twice."

Dad said, "I'm sure the boys would love it if their Aunt Timone would come along." He used the nickname my twin five-year-old nephews had given me when they were in their Lion King phase.

"What time are they going?" I asked, though I didn't particularly want to go. I loved my nephews more than life itself, but with my heart still in pieces, I didn't have it in me to be the fun-loving, cool aunt on this trip.

"What time is who going where?" Mom walked onto the patio. She was wearing navy capris and a red tank top. Her short gray hair was sticking out from under her wide-brimmed hat, and she had an overly bright smile on her face.

"Dad was saying that Naomi and her crew were heading to the Wright Brothers Memorial," I said.

Mom leaned against the wooden banister. "Oh, that will be fun. You girls used to love going there when you were kids. Why don't we just make it a family outing? There are a ton of great restaurants down there. We can order lunch and eat it at the park. We'll make a day of it."

Mom's eyes lit up, but my stomach tightened with dread. My mother lived for family vacations. Since I had moved to Richmond, and my sister's family had relocated to Colorado, this was the only time we were all under one roof. Each time I backed out of fun-filled-family-together-time, I felt as if I was letting my mother down, and I hated that feeling.

I started to reply when I felt Dad's calloused hand on my knee. "Elizabeth, why don't we let Simone decide what she wants to do *today*?"

Mom's eyes widened. "Oh, yes, yes, yes." Pity replaced recognition. "This is a day for her to choose what we do."

I sighed heavily, not missing that my mother had used the word "we" and not "she."

Thankfully, Dad came to the rescue. "I saw an advertisement in the paper about a spa that just opened in Kitty Hawk; I thought she may like to pamper herself." He pulled out his cell phone. "Is that something you would like, honey?"

I decided right then and there that I would never tease my father again about reading the local paper. I leaned over and kissed him on the cheek. "That sounds perfect, Dad."

Dad intentionally avoided Mom's gaze as he searched the paper for the number. "I'll set up the appointment."

"If you wait until tomorrow, your sister and I could go with you," Mom said.

"Elizabeth, I think Simone needs some time to herself," Dad replied.

Mom pressed her lips into a fine line. "Well, I guess I'll just go start breakfast then." She spun on her heel and marched toward the house.

When Mom was finally inside, Dad winked at me. "You know how kings of old used to have royal food tasters? I wonder how you get one of those. I think your Mom may try to slip some strychnine in my eggs."

"She'll be fine." I made a dismissive motion. "I just wish she would stop treating me like I am an eight-year-old who scraped her elbow."

"You gotta remember, kiddo, you'll always be her little girl." Dad stared out at the ocean. "There's nothing in the world worse than knowing your child is in pain and that you can't fix it."

"But I don't want her to fix it. This," I pointed to my chest, "can't be fixed. It will never be …" I choked back the sob rising in my throat.

"I know it feels that way."

I waited for him to finish with something like "but time heals all wounds" or "there are better fish in the sea," but he just let the statement hang in the salty air.

I turned away so he couldn't see the tear that had spilled onto my cheek. "Did you book the appointment with the spa?" I was desperate to change the subject.

"Not yet. I didn't know if you really wanted me to or if you just wanted an excuse to spend the afternoon by yourself." He took out his wallet and handed me his credit card. "But if you decide you want a massage or facial or whatever women do at those fancy places, it's on me." He pushed himself onto his feet. "I better go check on your Mom." He kissed me on the forehead. "See you inside."

~ ~ ~

That afternoon, as I watched my family pull away in my sister's Honda minivan, I had an unexplainable urge to run after them. Spending the afternoon alone had sounded so liberating this morning, but now that I stood all by myself in the driveway, alone didn't sound quite so appealing. That same sob that I'd choked down before rose in my chest.

"You're being melodramatic," I chastised myself. "They're going to a museum less than ten miles away, not leaving the country." I climbed the stairs to the upper deck of our rental home and stared at the ocean. Angry gray waves crashed on the sand. The red, no-swimming-allowed flags, snapped in the wind. The beach was practically deserted, just the way I liked it.

I grabbed a beach chair and the bag of books my sister had compiled for me. Then, I slipped on my flip flops and made my way to the shore.

At the water's edge, the white bubbles of broken waves kissed my toes. *Broken*, that word kept coming back to me. *Broken waves, broken shells, broken dreams.* I shook my head to clear the self-pity from my thoughts and unzipped the bag containing the books. My sister had deemed the collection the "How to get over a loser anthology." The first was *You are a Badass* by Jen Censero. Great theory, but I was looking for more of a distraction than self-help. Next was, *I am Malala* by Malala Yousafzia. Malala Yousafzi, the young girl who had been shot by the Taliban for demanding the right to be educated, was a personal hero of mine. I loved her story, but right now, I didn't have the emotional wherewithal for such a gut-wrenching tale.

I pulled a book from the bottom of the pile, hoping to find something less heavy. I was not disappointed. My sister had included my favorite author in the mix, Jennifer Weiner. As I read the opening page of *Goodnight Nobody*, I felt something brush against my foot. I looked down, expecting to see a shell or piece of driftwood. Instead, I saw a small, glass bottle floating in the shallow surf.

I picked up the bottle and shoved it into my bag as I grumbled about irresponsible tourists. Then I sat back in my beach chair and allowed myself to get lost in the drama of suburban housewifedom and murder.

After an hour of sitting in the sun, my body craved the air conditioning and maybe a mimosa. I returned to the house, and as I waited for the champagne to chill, I emptied the sand from my bag. The glass bottle that I'd collected rolled onto the counter. For the first time, I noticed that it wasn't just any bottle. The lid was still attached, and wax had been melted over the opening, like a Makers' Mark bottle of whiskey. Inside the bottle was a piece of paper.

"A message in a bottle?" I wondered out loud. Was my life really becoming a depressing Nicholas Sparks' novel? I removed the wax and lid then slammed the opening of the bottle against my palm until the paper came out. The paper was worn, but not old. I read the tidy, slanted handwriting:

Hello friend,

First things first, if you are reading this, it means one thing: my son is wrong. Zeke, it worked! Ha! You owe me a beer.

The second thing is that this bottle tells me what a speCial person yoU are. I prayed over this heRe letter and this heRe bottle. I prayed IT would be found by a soUl that needed Courage, Kindness, and hope. I pray that the little adventure I have laid out for you brings you these things.

My name is Karl. I am a retired NavaL officer who moved to the Outer Banks after my retirement in the early 90s. I have always been a lover of maps and treasure, so I hope you will entertain an old Gentleman in His quest To create a treasure map of His Own.

I have left a series of clUeS around the obx. I hopE you enjoy solving the puzzles as much as I enjoyed making THem. The clues are hIdden in plain sight. *This letteR is the first of four. The last will leaD you to a small treasure, at leaST I hope you find it to be A treasure.*

I hope you fInd youR reward,

Karl

I turned the paper over, expecting to see a rough, hand drawn picture of the area, but there was nothing. I peered into the bottle. "Where's the map?" I wondered aloud.

When I reread the letter, I realized it contained a code. Random letters were capitalized. I grabbed a pencil and a pad of paper. Then I wrote down every capitalized letter: -FCHYTCUIRRIIUCKMKINLOBIIGHTHOTUSEITHTTHRTDSTAIIR-

I tried to see a pattern, but absolutely nothing in the long string of letters could be arranged to make a coherent thought. I tried crossing out every second letter, then every third, but no message appeared. I studied the message until my head ached.

Just when I was ready to give up, I realized some of the letters that were capitalized followed common grammatical rules: they were at the first word of a sentence or the name of a place. Other capital letters were placed haphazardly.

I ignored letters that were supposed to be capitalized and focused on the random ones. -CURRITUCKLIGHTHOUSETHIRDSTAIR- I leaped to my feet, knocking over the barstool. "CURRITUCK LIGHTHOUSE THIRD STAIR!" I yelled into the empty house.

Currituck, a small village at the top of the barrier islands that made up the Outer Banks, was a hidden-in-plain-sight gem. I checked my phone to make sure the light house was open for tours then hopped in my car and headed north.

I arrived at the Currituck Beach Lighthouse just after two. The magnificent redbrick structure towered into the sky, creating a beautiful contrast with the gray clouds. Unlike the more popular destinations of Hatteras or Bodie Island, the Currituck Lighthouse didn't get the tourist attention it deserved. I paid $10 for my ticket at the front door of the lighthouse and began my search for the mysterious third stair.

Immediately inside the door was a short hallway with a black and white checkerboard floor. At the end of the hallway, was a small cement staircase. I made sure nobody was looking, then got down on my knees and inspected the third stair. There was no hidden message, no secret compartment, and no hidden bottles. At the top of the stairs, the stairway split into two smaller stairwells. Again, I got on my hands and knees and carefully inspected every inch of the third stair. After getting some pretty weird looks and obtrusive questions, I moved on to the metal spiral staircase that led to the top of the lighthouse.

As I repeated my thorough inspection of every third stair I could find, I felt a tap on my shoulder. A woman in a brown khaki shirt and green shorts was staring at me, a deep v between her furrowed brows. "Can I help you, ma'am?"

Blood rushed to my face. I felt foolish enough for believing a stupid message in a bottle, but to admit it to another human being was too much. "No, I'm just, just admiring the architecture."

The lady nodded, but her body language communicated her true thoughts: This lady is coo-coo.

Then an idea hit me. "Is there a bar around here or an outbuilding that is named 'The Third Stair?'"

"The third stair?" The ranger cocked her head to the side. "Was that why you were inspecting the steps?"

Now, I felt like a full-fledged idiot. Tears burned my eyes. I had to get out of there. I lowered my head and prepared to make a beeline for the exit. "I'm sorry," I muttered as I passed by the woman.

To my shock, I felt a strong hand grab my elbow. "Did you say the third stair?"

I kept my head down. "I'm sorry for being a nuisance."

Her grip on my elbow tightened. "I need you to follow me."

Shit, I thought. I had gotten so caught up on the ideas of treasure and lore, that it never once occurred to me that this could have been a devious plot by drug smugglers or human traffickers. Had I intercepted a communication between a supplier and distributor? Would the state police be waiting for me when I got to the ranger station? How was I going to explain this to my parents? I couldn't afford a lawyer! I was too soft to do hard time!

My feet felt as if they were encased in concrete as I allowed the woman to lead me out of the lighthouse and into the red brick building next door.

"Have a seat," she said, then walked through a door that said: Employees Only.

I eyed the door. I could run for it. Well, I mean I could probably run for like a hundred yards. Damn it, why hadn't I gotten in better shape for the wedding? I should have done one of those couch-to-5k programs or something.

When the woman returned to the room, a man with a long gray beard and matching outfit followed. "Christine told me you were looking for the third stair." The man gave me a good once over.

I held up my hands. "I swear I'm not a drug runner!" The words shot out of my mouth before I could stop them.

The rangers exchanged a confused look.

So that hadn't worked. I tried to explain again. "This is a mistake. I found a message in a bottle. It washed up on shore. I swear, I'm not doing anything illegal."

The man cocked his head to the side. "A coded message that read Currituck Lighthouse Third Stair?"

"I swear, I just thought it was a local having fun with a tourist. I didn't mean..." Something inside my brain clicked. "Wait, did you just say Currituck Lighthouse Third Stair?" How did he know what the message said?

The man blew out a long breath. "Some time ago, a retired Naval officer came to the lighthouse. He said if anybody ever came and asked about the third stair, I was to give them this." He handed me a manila envelope. "I'm Logan, by the way."

My hand shook as I reached out and grabbed the envelope. "Thank you."

The female ranger studied me with curious eyes. "So, you literally found a message in a bottle that told you to come here?"

I nodded.

"That's so freaking cool!"

Once it became obvious that I wasn't going to be hauled off to the jail, my heart rate began to return to normal. The gentleman made me coffee as I explained everything that had happened since I found the message. I pulled the original parchment from my purse. He held it in his hands as if it were a piece of bone China.

"I've lived on the shore for almost sixty-five years. This is truly something special." He handed the paper back to me.

Christin was bouncing up and down on the balls of her feet "Well, are you going to open it?" She nodded at the new envelope.

Logan gave her a reproachful side eye, but I made a dismissive motion. "She's fine. I'd actually appreciate a set of local eyes on the clues."

I sat in the folding black chair and slid open the envelope's seal. My hands were shaking as I removed the paper, though this time it was from excitement and not fear of being mistaken for a drug runner.

The same neat, slanted handwriting that was on the original letter was on this stationery as well.

Hello friend,

I am so very excited that you found the second clue. I hope you enjoyed the trip to Corolla. It is my favorite beach in North Carolina and one of the ones least affected by the passage of time.

The Outer Banks have changed so much since my Loraine and I moved to the area. As I said in my original letter, I am a retired Naval officer. I spent twenty-three years dragging my family around the globe, and so when I was finishing up my career in Virginia, I told Loraine she got to choose where we lived next. She didn't think I could live in more than one place for more than four years, so on a Dare we bought a house on the coast of North Carolina. I've been here twenty-two years.

We've watched the pristine shores go from barren dunes to vacation homes, to an all-out tourist destination. Towns like Kitty Hawk used to resemble Mayberry, but now they are filled with chain stores and tourist shops.

But that's enough lamenting from an old coot.

Lorraine and I had a long and fulfilling marriage. After fighting cancer for the third time, her heart wore out. She went to be with the Lord last spring. I miss my Bell every day, but I am so thankful for the life we had together. She was my best friend. We have a beautiful son, Zeke, the one who said that leaving a message in a bottle was foolishness. (Who's foolish now, son?)

These islands have been good to me. The saltwater helped me heal the wounds of two foreign conflicts. They sheltered me from hurricanes and saw my hair turn gray. Now they are the balm healing the heart of a widower missing the love of his life.

I hear my Loraine in the whisper of the waves. I see her smile in the red sunrise, and I am at peace.

I hope that the salt and the sand is as good to your soul as it is to mine.

Karl

I wiped the tears that had fallen onto my cheeks. Karl and Loraine's story brought me such joy and pain. To know that love like that existed was beautiful, but the fact that it always seemed just beyond my reach sliced my heart.

I handed the letter to Logan and Christine. "You guys have any idea what this clue means?"

They took turns reading the letter then returned it to me. "Not a clue, but this Karl guy's right," Logan said. "The beach has changed a lot over the years."

I looked at him with saucer-wide eyes. "You don't think the clues have been destroyed by developers, do you?"

He pointed to the paper in my hands. "It has only been a year or so since the old sailor came here to give me that clue. I can't think of anything that's gone away in the past year."

I let out a sigh of relief, then reread the letter. "Now if only I had an idea where to start."

Logan tugged on his beard. "How about this, I'll noodle on it a while, too. If you're fine with giving me your number, I'll shoot you a text if I think of anything."

Though I wasn't in the habit of giving my number to a complete stranger, I was so intrigued by this quest that I threw caution to the wind.

As I was walking out the door, Logan said, "Would you mind letting me know if you find the next clue? I'm intrigued by this whole thing."

I gave him a wink. "Sure thing."

I hadn't even made it to my car before Logan texted me: **Still working on the clue. Let me know if you find anything.**

~ ~ ~

I was lounging on the couch studying the letter when the crew arrived home. Mom was the first through the door. "We stopped at the Kill Devil's Grill to grab lunch. I picked up your usual."

I hid the letter in my pocket and pushed myself to my feet. "Crab cakes and key lime pie?" I asked.

Mom winked at me. "I know what my girl needs."

I couldn't help but think she was talking about more than just lunch.

As we sat down at the oversized table, my nephews recounted their trip to the Wright Brothers Memorial. Bentley was sitting in my lap. "You can see the entire island from the monument, the ocean, and the sound! And on the day of the first flight, they set up a camera. There is an actual picture of the plane on display!" He hopped off my lap, spread his arms wide and began making whooshing sounds as he circled the dining room.

Not to be outdone, Brayden stood on the back of the sofa with a blanket draped around his shoulders. "Did you know that the wood that built the first plane was from Papaw's hometown?" He leaped from his spot and barrel rolled into the kitchen.

I looked at Naomi. "How in the world do you keep up with these two? I'm exhausted just watching them."

She shrugged. "Mostly Prozac and coffee."

Her husband, Chris, rolled his eyes. "Eventually, you're going to have to stop making that joke in front of the boys."

"Who's joking? Being a boy-Mom isn't for the faint of heart."

I looked to my nephews, who were now taking turns attempting to suplex one another. "Well, my day probably wasn't nearly as exciting as yours."

Mom reached for the salt. "How was the spa?"

Dad and I locked eyes. I'd forgotten about our spa cover story. "I, ah, canceled the appointment. I just didn't feel like spending time around strangers today."

"Or family either," Mom mumbled under her breath.

I bit the inside of my cheek to keep from giving a smart aleck reply. "I did have an adventure of my own, though."

"You did?" Naomi jumped in to change the subject. "What did you get yourself into?"

I launched into the story about finding the message on the beach, my trip to the Currituck Lighthouse, and receiving the second clue. I pulled the two letters from my pocket and handed them to my sister. Dad and Chris read the clues over her shoulder, but Mom stood rooted in her spot with her arms crossed over her chest.

"You went all by yourself? How do you know it wasn't some trap? Did you know that the top demographic for kidnapping victims for human trafficking are white women in their mid-twenties?"

I rolled my eyes. "I think if somebody were trying to abduct me, they wouldn't have left a clue directing me to a popular tourist attraction."

"Still, I think you should have spoken to one of us before you went gallivanting off and—"

"And what, Mom?! Before visiting a lighthouse without your permission? For wanting to be alone on the day I was all but stood up at the altar? For wanting to be treated like an adult?"

I could tell from her audible gasp that my words had wounded her, but I didn't care. I pushed myself to my feet, knocking over my cane-back chair.

The boys stopped wrestling at the crash. Brayden looked at me with wide eyes. "What's wrong, Aunt Timone?"

"I'm fine. I just need some space," I muttered as I stormed out the door.

After a good five minutes of stomping around the deck, I heard the screen door open and close. I looked up to see my dad walking toward me.

"How ya doing, kiddo?"

I gave him a sideways glare. "How do you think I'm doing?"

"You were pretty hard on your Mom back there." He slid into one of the Adirondack chairs. "Ya know, she's doing the best she knows how. It's rough for her."

"Rough for her?" I threw my hands in the air. "Right now, I should be making a cheesy champagne toast, eating cake, and dancing to some sappy love song! Instead, I'm getting a guilt trip about not wanting to get pedicures! I finally found something to take my mind off the shitshow that is my life, and I'm supposed to put HER feelings first!"

Dad's jaw tightened, and I knew I was close to crossing that invisible line. "You don't have to put her feelings first, but it's not alright for you to act as if she doesn't have any feelings."

I dropped my head and softened my tone. "I know she is trying, and I appreciate it. But Mom has never experienced anything like this. You two started dating when you were seventeen. She found the love of her life before she was even out of high school. She doesn't know what it feels like to build your entire life around someone just to have them betray you." I collapsed into the wooden chair beside my dad and buried my face in my hands. "She just doesn't get it."

"I think she gets it more than you realize."

When the weight of his words hit me, my blood chilled in my veins. My head shot up, and I glared at my father. "You didn't!"

He held up his palms in defense. "I was never unfaithful to your mother, but that's not to say I was the best husband in the world either."

"You two have the perfect marriage."

Dad gave a silent chuckle. "Your mother always used to say that the Navy was my wife, and that she was my mistress. She said it in a joking manner, but I knew there was a painful kernel of truth under the surface."

"I thought Mom liked being a military wife."

"She wasn't just a military wife; she was an officer's wife. It comes with an unwritten contract of obligations and duties. Not only did she have to keep the home fires burning while I was away, but she was also a mentor to many of the other wives on base."

I'd never thought about my mom like that, thousands of miles from home, raising two young kids. Adding the stress of being the one young wives looked to, it must have been crippling. I stared out at the ocean. "She seemed to always handle it effortlessly."

"That she did." The lines around his eyes crinkled when he smiled. "You and your sister never saw what Elizabeth had to give up."

"What did she give up?"

Dad exhaled heavily. "Your Mom was so driven when we were in college. She graduated Summa Cum Lade with a degree in business and advertising."

"Wait, she didn't get her degree in education?"

"Not until much later. Teaching was one of the few careers possible for a military spouse to have, but it wasn't her dream. She wanted to do graphic design for a huge magazine, designing ads that inspired and empowered women. But to work your way up in a corporation like that takes time and dedication, twice as much when you're a woman. When you have to move every four years because of your spouse's job..." He rubbed the stubble on his chin. "Your mother realized her passion for advertising would never come to fruition, so you and your sister became her passion. She made sure you and Naomi never wanted for anything, emotionally, spiritually, or physically. She was there for every practice, every PTA meeting, every performance. She fixed your lunches; she fixed your clarinets; she fixed your boo boos. Now that there is something she can't fix, she doesn't know how to handle it."

I motioned to my chest. "She can't fix this. I have to endure it. I have to be the one to experience the pain; I have to be the one to mourn."

"Have you tried telling your Mom that?"

I looked out at the crashing waves. "It would just hurt her feelings."

Dad shrugged. "No worse than you being in a constant battle with her." He put his hand on my knee. "This entire week, your Mom has been racking her brain, trying to be what you need her to be. Why don't you try telling her what you need her to be? She may just surprise you."

I winked at Dad. "How did you get to be so wise?"

He winked back. "I'm married to a pretty amazing woman."

I stayed on the deck for a few minutes and thought about what my dad had said. When I walked back into the kitchen, I was quite surprised to find the adults gathered around the dining room table with the two letters from Karl set out before them.

"So, which one was in the bottle?" Naomi asked.

I took the seat beside my sister. "The one with the random capitalizations."

Mom picked up the parchment and studied it. "Oh, yes, I see now. If you ignore the words that were supposed to be capitalized, you can clearly see Currituck Lighthouse spelled out." She put the paper back on the table. "Although, I'm not surprised you figured it out, Simone. You've always been so clever."

I could see that this was an olive branch, and I gladly accepted. "I guess it's in the genes."

Naomi asked, "Do you have any ideas about the second message?"

I shrugged. "Not really. The first one had obvious letters that stood out. This one only has one capitalized letter that doesn't belong. The D in dare, and I assumed it was to emphasize how much Loraine disbelieved he couldn't settle down."

Dad picked up the paper. "It has to be a clue."

Chris looked over Dad's shoulder. "Aren't we in Dare County?"

I slapped my forehead. "Duh. The next clue is probably in Dare County!"

"He also mentions that they were stationed in Virginia when they made the decision." Mom slipped her iPhone from her back pocket. "Virginia Dare was the first white settler born in the new world." She started tapping on her phone. "She was a member of The Lost Colony on Roanoke Island."

Something clicked inside my brain. "I remember watching an episode of *Expeditions Unknown* with Josh Gates. While supply ships went back to England, the entire colony just disappeared. Nobody knows what happened to them."

Dad drummed his fingers on the table. "Liz, do you remember that play we watched down there about ten years ago. It had all those amazing costumes. Wasn't that on Roanoke Island?"

"Now that you mention it, I believe it was." She tapped on her phone some more, and a gigantic smile spread across her face. "And you will never guess who does the voiceover at the beginning of the play?"

"Who?" Naomi and I asked in unison.

Mom held out her phone so that it was facing us. "None other than Andy Griffith, who played the sheriff of —-"

"Mayberry!" we all answered.

Chris slapped the table. "The next clue is at that theater."

"I bet you're right!" Naomi patted him on the back.

"Well, I guess we'll head to Roanoke Island tomorrow to find out." Mom looked at me warily. "That is, if you want company."

I smiled. "I'd love company."

~ ~ ~

The next morning, I left a note for my family when I walked to the ocean to watch the sun rise. I didn't receive any worried notifications on my watch, so I took my time walking along the waves. When my stomach let out a monstrous growl, I headed back toward the house.

Naomi and Chris were feeding the boys on the deck when I made it to the last step.

"How ya' feeling this morning, sis?" Naomi asked.

"I guess pretty good, for the day after the day I was supposed to get married."

Chris nodded to me. "At least you didn't wake up hungover."

Naomi handed Brayden a piece of pancake. "At least you didn't wake up next to a narcissistic man-child."

I sat across from the boys at the picnic table. "I guess you have a point there." I looked at the boys. "So, what is on the agenda today for two strapping young lads? The lifeguards were putting up red flags again; I don't think we'll see much beach time."

Bentley shoved a fist full of cheerios into his mouth. "We're going to a pirate museum and to an aquarium. They have real, killer sharks."

Chris rolled his eyes. "Turns out Roanoke Island has a children's museum and the North Carolina Aquarium. Your dad and I are going to lead the boys on an adventure while the women folk go on your treasure hunt."

"No fair!" Bentley whined. "I want to go on a treasure hunt!"

I bopped him on the nose. "This isn't that kind of treasure hunt. There's no gold doubloons or booty. We're on a quest for information."

Bentley stuck out his tongue. "That sounds boring; I'd rather see pirates." He picked up the closest fork. "Hand over your loot, ye landlubbers." With that, the boys began a tabletop swashbuckling fight that resulted in spilled orange juice.

I pushed myself onto my feet. "I'm going to go grab some coffee."

"Take me with you!" Chris called after me.

~ ~ ~

After lunch, Dad, Chris, and the boys loaded into the minivan, while Mom, Naomi and I climbed into my SUV. As soon as I turned onto US 12 South, Naomi fell asleep in the back seat, and Mom stared out the passenger window. I thought about the things Dad had told me yesterday, how she'd sacrifice her dreams and career so he could become a high-ranking officer and how she had made my sister and me her passion. It was the first time I'd ever looked at my mom with pity.

"Mom," I put my hand on her knee. "I'm sorry you had to give up your dreams."

She turned from the window and looked at me as if I had five heads. "What on earth are you talking about?"

"Dad told me last night you couldn't pursue your chosen path of advertising, so you built your life around his career, Naomi, and me."

"I built my life around you three," she scoffed. "Somebody certainly has a high opinion of themself."

I couldn't tell if she was talking about Dad or me, but whichever it was, she was not regarding them kindly. I tried not to get defensive. "Yesterday, Dad told me —"

"What, that I'd given up my dreams so he could climb the ranks? That I was a poor pitiful housewife while he was off having adventures?"

Her tone took me completely off guard. "Wait, he said you wanted to go into advertising but couldn't because you had to move so often."

Mom rolled her eyes. "Your father has always felt guilty for," she made air quotes, "dragging me around the world"."

"He said you had to make sacrifices."

She made a dismissive motion. "You make sacrifices no matter who your spouse is."

Considering that today I was supposed to wake up as "a spouse" and hadn't, it was hard for me to find an appropriate reply. So, I asked another question, "What did Dad sacrifice for you?"

Mom shrugged. "His salary is what put me through college. He retired at twenty years instead of going for twenty-five because I wanted to be close to my parents. He gave up opportunities to further his career because it would have meant time away from the family. It was give-and-take, regardless of what your father says. Not to mention, having a spouse in the Navy had a lot of benefits." She got a wistful look in her eyes. "I loved living all around the globe. We celebrated our ten-year anniversary in Santorini. I got to teach you and your sister how to swim in the crystal blue waters of Hanalei. I celebrated my thirtieth birthday on a cruise around Gibraltar." A puckish smile spread across her face. "That was an evening to remember."

"Dad said you used to complain that the Navy was his first wife, and you were his mistress."

"I won't lie. Sometimes it did feel like that." Mom shook her head. "There were times that I didn't like the lifestyle. And there were times we fought about the sacrifices I had to make, but every couple fights."

I furrowed my brow. "So, you're not bitter that you didn't have a career?"

"Didn't have a career?" Her voice rose an octave, and her cheeks turned magenta. "Are you implying teaching isn't a career?"

"No, that's not what I mean." Why was she getting so bent out of shape about this? All I was trying to do was thank her for her sacrifices, and she was acting like I was insulting her. I gripped the wheel tighter. "Just forget about it."

But that door had been opened, and, by damn, my mother was going to walk through. "I have two bachelor's degrees and a master's. I spent thirty-two years teaching math and computer programming. I've taught children of dignitaries and future congress women. Are you telling me that is not a career?"

"Mom, can we drop it? I'm sorry, okay?"

But she was on a roll. "Just because I wasn't in some corporate office doesn't mean I didn't have a powerful career." There was something other than indignation in her voice. Frustration? Hurt? Years of being devalued?

She stared straight ahead, and when she spoke again, her voice was calm and level. "Society will tell you that only those who head corporations or handle huge accounts have power, but they don't understand power. The greatest power in life is to empower others. There were girls in my math classes who honestly thought a woman was incapable of doing complex equations. They are now engineers, computer programmers, and professors. I taught a young man who thought that his only choice in life was to follow in the footsteps of his alcoholic father. He's now a surgeon. I didn't build my life around others; I used my life to build others up." There was a steel edge to her voice. "Do not ever mistake service for weakness."

I thought back over the years, the mailboxes full of Christmas cards from former students, the birth announcements, the time my mom was asked to sit in the mother-of-the-bride chair. These were all powerful things, maybe not power the way Wall Street or even society sees it, but power, nonetheless. "I'm sorry, Mom. You're right. I guess I never realized just how much power a teacher has."

Mom nodded. "Power to build up, or the power to tear down. I've seen those in my profession do both. I had both done to me when I was a student."

It occurred to me she seldom talked about her own school days, the days when she taught, yes, but I knew very little about when she was a student. Suddenly, I wanted to know everything. "What were you like in high school?"

"I was quite a bit like you, bright yet misguided, outspoken and stubborn, strong, empathetic, and vulnerable." She gave a soft laugh.

"And that's when you met Dad?" I knew the story. They had senior English together, and Dad bugged her until she went out with him. It was a story so tooth-rotting sweet, the Hallmark Channel would have looked at it and said, "That's just too cheesy."

"I met your dad in twelfth grade. Sometimes, I wish I'd met him earlier, it would have prevented a lot of heartaches."

"Were there other guys before Dad?" I'd never heard about any of this. In fact, I had always just assumed my mom was completely chaste before meeting my father.

"Yes."

"Any significant?"

Mom shrugged. "Significant is a relative term, but there are ones I remember, ones I regret."

"Tell me about them?" I don't know why I asked. Perhaps if I could hear about her own missteps and broken hearts, it would make me feel better about my own.

Mom stared out the windshield then began to speak. "In my tenth-grade year, I fell really hard for a boy who had just moved to our school. He didn't feel the same way about me, but he liked the feeling of my adoration. Every time I started to move on and be interested in someone else, a tragedy would befall him. I'd get a teary phone call, where he would describe how his world was falling apart. He'd tell me I was the only one who believed in him, how there'd be nothing to live for without me."

I thought about the beginning of my relationship with Trevor. It sounded as if Mom was telling me MY story. I gripped the wheel tighter as she continued.

"When he'd move on to another girl, I'd be heartbroken. I'd swear I was done with him, but when he came back, I was there waiting with open arms. I needed to feel needed. He saw that in me, and he exploited it. Eventually, I found myself evolving into somebody I didn't know or like very much." She chewed her bottom lip.

"How did you break free?" I wasn't just asking because I wanted to know her story; I sincerely needed to know how to break the spell that had been cast over me.

"It was actually a teacher who helped with that." The corners of her mouth turned up in a warm smile. "My home economics teacher was taking a group of us to a competition on the other side of the state. It was a six-hour drive, so there was a lot of time to chat. We talked about everything from my future plans, to how she grew up, to her kids. When I started talking to her about this boy, she actually listened. Everybody else had treated me like a silly girl with a crush, but she made me feel like my emotions were real and that they mattered."

"She sounds amazing."

A nostalgic smile spread across Mom's face. "She was. I poured out my heart; I told her how much I loved that boy; how he made me feel when he said he needed me; how nobody understood but me."

"Did she tell you that he was using you?" I asked.

"No, she just gave me a sideways glance and said, 'seems like he needs you the most just when you are ready to walk away. I wonder who he turns to all those other times?'" Mom touched her temple. "Finally, something clicked. I saw the situation for what it was." She turned to look at me. "If she'd badmouthed him, like everybody else, I would have rushed to his defense. But she was a wise woman. She knew that I had to come to the conclusion on my own."

A revelation washed over me like a cold wave. Though I had never admitted it to myself, I resented my mom for not warning me about Trevor. I was angry at her for not protecting me, but now I saw it. She had a wisdom that was beyond my understanding. She knew I had to come to the realization on my own.

I could no longer stop the tears. For so long I had underestimated the woman sitting beside me. I had resented her; I had looked down on her, I had been downright mean to her. Now, I was in utter awe of her. She was wise; she was worldly; she was powerful; she was passionate; she was a force to be reckoned with… she was my mother.

Mom reached over and wiped a tear from my cheek. "What's wrong Simone?"

I pulled her hand to my mouth and kissed it. "Absolutely nothing, Mom. Absolutely nothing."

~ ~ ~

When we finally arrived at The Waterside Theater, I was captivated by its beauty. The three thousand seat, open-air amphitheater with the blue waters of the sound as its backdrop was simply majestic.

"I can't believe we never came here before." Naomi stood between Mom and me. "It's breathtaking."

"It is." I scanned the stage and seating area. "But, where in the world do we start looking for the next clue?"

Mom asked, "Did you bring the letters with you?"

I pulled the two pieces of paper from my purse. "Got them right here."

We reread the letters and began traipsing around the area. After an hour of looking under seats, in the limbs of trees, and behind shrubs, we were hot, tired, and confused. Mom plopped down in the front row. "Where on earth can it be?"

"Let me see those letters." Naomi pulled the papers from my hands. Her eyebrows furrowed as she read, then suddenly she yelled, "I think I know." She sprinted to the back of the amphitheater. Mom and I ran after her. By the time we caught up to her, she was standing in front of a cement marker.

"What in the world?" I panted.

"Bell." Naomi pointed to the second letter. "I thought it was a term of endearment for his late wife. However, belle, as in French for beauty, is spelled with an 'e.'"

Mom cocked her head to the side. "So, he's a bad speller?"

A smile spread over Naomi's face. "I thought so too, then I saw this." She pointed to the marker in front of us. "Albert Quinten Bell was the man who singlehandedly built and saved this theater. The next clue has to be here!" She got down on her hands and knees and began digging in the mulch. I joined her in the digging while Mom kept watch for park rangers.

Just when I was ready to give up, Naomi let out a loud, "Wee Hoo!" She held up a green, glass bottle with a wax covered cork.

"That looks just like the first bottle!" I squealed.

"Here, I'll open it." My mom ripped the bottle from my hands, removed the cork, and unrolled the paper from inside.

Hello friend,

Congratulations for making it this far. You are a mighty treasure hunter and an intelligent sleuth. I hope you have a chance to catch the show. The costumes are truly amazing, the story is engaging, and you won't find better talent on Broadway.

This theater was a favorite for Loraine and me. She was my angel; my shelter in the storm; my saving Grace. Our love was real, not like you read about in those horrendous paperback, romance novels. After my tours in Korea, she was my safe shelter, my life-saving refuge. I would spend hours in the waves, letting the saltwater wash away the memories that haunted me. This poor, fainting, struggling seaman will forever be thankful that I married such an angel.

In the morning, we'd walk along the shoreline. We held hands, and we collected shells. I only wanted to collect the ones that were whole, but Loraine always reminded me that there was a unique beauty in brokenness.

She was a wise woman.

So, this is the final clue to my treasure hunt. If you can decipher this jumble and find your way to the destination, treasure awaits you.

Peace be with you,

Karl

Mom, Naomi, and I passed the letter back and forth. "Any ideas?" I asked.

Naomi shook her head. "Not a single one."

Mom furrowed her brow. "Nothing is jumping out at me either. Perhaps we should let your father and Chris look at this."

"Oh, no, no, no. I'm not just handing this off to the menfolk." I crossed my arms over my chest.

Mom pursed her lips. "It doesn't have to be a competition. Besides, I think your father is really enjoying the adventure."

I knew she was right, but part of me liked the fact that the three Craig women had found the clue all by ourselves. I wanted to save it, make it just our own. However, I was keenly aware that we had a looming deadline. Soon, our week at the beach would be over, and my opportunity to solve the mystery would dissolve. "I guess we can include the guys."

Naomi put her hand on my shoulder. "Let's find a place for dinner. We can discuss and Google over margaritas."

I cocked my head to the side. "I thought you were a wine person. Since when do you have such a fondness for tequila?"

"Since I started raising five-year-old, twin boys."

~ ~ ~

At dinner, while Brayden and Bentley rattled on and on about swabbing the deck and finding treasure upon the Elizabeth II, Dad and Chris took their turns trying to decipher Karl's clues.

"Any ideas?" I asked when the boys finally took a breath.

Dad rubbed the graying stubble on his chin. "I got nothing."

"Me either." Chris shrugged.

We tossed ideas back and forth until it was time to head back to the theater for the show. We sat near the back so that if the boys got antsy, we wouldn't disturb other viewers, but it was a nonissue. They were completely enraptured by the tales of the first white settlers to arrive in the Americas. They fell asleep on the ride back to Duck. In fact, all of us were pretty tuckered out by our day of adventure.

That night was the first time in three weeks where I didn't cry myself to sleep. Instead, I read and reread Karl's words. In these few short letters, I could feel his devotion to Loraine and hers to him. That was the kind of love that I wanted. That was the kind of love that I deserved! Trevor never would have loved me like that. He was too busy planning "the next thing" to ever worry about my dreams. I thought about my own parents, how Mom and Dad had worked together to make each other's dreams come true. I thought about their wisdom and the experiences I'd been too stubborn or proud to ask about.

I put the letters away, and for the first time since college, I thought about my dreams, my desires. Finally, I drifted off into a content sleep.

~ ~ ~

The following morning, I asked my mom to come with me on my morning walk. She and I walked along the breaking zone, picking up the most beautiful shell fragments. "I'm thinking about taking a class on mosaics at the senior center. I think that these would be beautiful, don't you, Simone?"

I looked at the brown, black, and gray fragments in her hands. I could envision them taking shape; their brokenness bound together into a new and artistic form. "I think it would be beautiful."

When we got back to the house, Chris and Naomi were getting the boys slathered with sunscreen. "How were the waves this morning?" Chris asked.

"Much tamer than the last two days. The flags are yellow, but I think it would be safe to do some wave riding."

"Are you going to boogie board with us, Aunt Timone?" Brayden asked.

I ruffled his hair. "Yep."

Bentley jumped up and down. "Really, you're actually coming with us!"

I bent down so that I was eye to eye with the twins. "I'm going to find the biggest, baddest wave in the Atlantic, and leave you in my wake." Then I ran inside the house, changed into my bathing suit, and met the family back on the patio. I winked at the boys. "You two ready to eat my bubbles?"

We spent the entire morning building sandcastles, riding the waves, and burying one another in the sand. By lunchtime, we were all hot, hungry, and sandy.

While the boys jumped into the pool, I snuck to the kitchen to take another look at the letters. Not to my surprise, Dad and Naomi already had them out on the dining room table rereading the clues.

Dad wrinkled his forehead. "I keep coming back to the last paragraph: *She was my angel; my shelter in the storm; my saving Grace. Our love was real, not like you read about in those horrendous paperback, romance novels. After my tours in Korea, she was my safe shelter, my life-saving refuge.*" He pointed at the letter. "The line about the paperback romance novels seems so out of place with the rest of his prose."

Naomi slapped her forehead with her hand. "How could I have been so stupid?!" She picked her phone and said as she typed. "Nicholas Sparks, set one of his romance novels in the Outer Banks." A smug smile spread across her face. "*Nights in Rodanthe.*"

"Isn't Rodanthe right above Hatteras?" I felt my heart race.

Naomi tapped more on her phone. Her smug smile turned into an all-out grin. "And guess what else is in Rodanthe?"

I grabbed the phone out of her hand. My eyes tripled in size when I read the screen. "The Chicamacomico Life-Saving Station Museum." I smiled so big my cheeks hurt. "Naomi, you are a genius!"

Naomi blew onto her nails and wiped them on her shirt. "It's a blessing and a curse."

We pulled the boys reluctantly from the pool, got quick showers then, piled in the minivan and headed south. Forty-five minutes later, we arrived at the Chicamacomico Life-Saving Station Museum. Men in white, old-fashioned uniforms moved in formations on the museum grounds.

"What's going on?" asked Brayden.

Naomi checked her phone. "This says on every Thursday there is a reenactment of a rescue."

"We want to see! We want to see!" The twins had already unbuckled their seatbelts.

Chris, who was sitting with Mom and Dad in the third row of the van, raised his hand. "I'll take the boys. You four investigate."

While Chris and the boys headed toward the reenactment, the rest of the crew headed toward the exhibits. The museum was quaint and well preserved, with restored boathouses and historically accurate living quarters. Though Dad, the retired Navy man, had to be pried away from each exhibit, the women of the crew quickly scanned the displays, anxious to find anything that would lead us to the final clue. Fifteen minutes after we entered *The 1874 Station,* we heard Dad yell, "Simone, bring that letter here."

I followed my father's voice until I found him staring at a small wooden plaque with a two-stanza poem burned into the orange wood.

Dad read the words aloud, "Trim your feeble lamp, my brother. Some pour sailor tempest tos't. Trying now to reach the harbor, in the darkness, may be lost. Let the lower lights be burning, send a gleam across the wave--- Some pour fainting struggling seaman. You may rescue! You may save!"

He began humming a melodic tune. "I knew I recognized those words. It's a song that we used to sing at the close of council circle when I was in 4-H."

"What does that have to do with the letter?" I asked.

He held the letter up to the plaque and pointed to the last paragraph. "Look at this line: *Some poor fainting struggling seaman* are both in the letter and burned into the plaque."

I covered my mouth with my hand. "This must be the final clue."

"You're right!" Naomi bounced up and down on the balls of her feet. "We found it! We found the final clue!"

"But what does it mean?" Mom asked.

I reached out to lift the plaque, to see if there was a message behind it. Then, I heard a gruff voice behind me. "Please don't touch the exhibit."

I spun around, ready to be reprimanded. Then, a huge smile spread across my face. A bald man with a long white beard wearing a park ranger's uniform stood in front of me.

"Logan!" I motioned from the man to my family. "Mom, Dad, Naomi. This is Logan. He's the one who gave me the envelope at the Currituck Light—"

Logan jabbed a calloused finger in my direction. "You were supposed to text me and let me know when you found the next clue." He rubbed his bald head. "This throws a monkey wrench into things, Simone. Why didn't you keep in contact?" His eyes were neither menacing nor friendly, but his tone sent a chill up my spine.

My father stepped in between us. "Just who are you?"

"I've had to have somebody watching every clue point, keeping tabs on you." Logan took a step to the left so that he could continue to stare me down. "You don't realize how important it is that we be here for this."

"We?" Out of the corner of my eye, I saw a second man appear at the doorway of the room. He was younger, in his early thirties. He wore pressed khakis and a pink polo. "I'll take it from here." He turned to look at me. The corners of his mouth turned up in a casual smile. "We have been waiting for you for a long time."

My mind ping-ponged back and forth between terror and confusion. Who was this guy and what did he have planned for me and my family? Was this a hidden camera thing? Were we about to become reality TV stars? Were they murderers? Were we about to become the feature on the five o'clock news?

Logan glared at the new guy. "I want to be the one who gives her what she deserves."

"Uncle Logan," the younger man raised his voice. "I think you're scaring them."

Naomi threw her hands in the air. "Can somebody please tell me what is going on?"

The younger man stepped forward. "I'm Zeke, and this is my uncle, Logan." He pointed to the piece of paper in my hand. "And it seems you have solved my father's treasure map."

"Zeke?" His words unwound themselves in my brain. "Karl and Loraine's Zeke?"

He tilted his head to the side. "You speak of my parents as if you knew them."

I held out the letter in a shaking hand. "I know it may sound crazy, but I feel as if I do."

"No crazier than starting a treasure hunt with a message in a bottle." Logan crossed his arms over his chest. "That brother of mine always had a flair for the dramatic."

"Wait, wait, wait." My mother pulled her phone from her purse and typed what I assumed was 911. "Karl, the man who wrote the letters, is your brother and your father, but he didn't show up. Instead, you two, after having your minions follow us all over the islands, show up." She pointed to Logan and Zeke respectively.

"Mom, I don't think they mean us any harm." I put my hand on her shoulder. "I think if they meant to harm us, they wouldn't have lured us to a public museum."

Mom didn't soften. She glared at the two men. "Then tell me, why are you two here and not Karl?"

A flicker of pain crossed over Zeke's face. "Dad passed away a week after he finished the fourth letter. That was about six months ago." His Adam's apple bobbed up and down as he swallowed. "We put the bottle in the ocean when we scattered his ashes."

Logan wiped his eyes. "He was the best brother in the world. And you wouldn't even let me be a part of the treasure hunt that was his last adventure."

I realized what I originally thought was aggression was sadness. "I'm sorry, Logan. Why didn't you tell me?"

"I gave you my number; I thought that was telling enough." He made a dismissive motion with his hand. "Probably better this way. If you'd known Karl was my brother, you'd probably have wanted my help in deciphering the clues. He wanted the searcher to be the one to figure it out."

Naomi interjected, "And you've had people keeping tabs on us as we searched for the clues?"

Logan pointed to his ranger shirt. "I have eyes and ears all over the Outer Banks."

Zeke turned his attention to me. "Dad knew his days were short; and he wanted to leave something behind. So, he devised the treasure map. He passed right after he finished the last note." Zeke pointed to the letter in my hand. "As Dad mentioned, I didn't think it would work. Looks like he got to prove me wrong one last time."

A lump formed in my throat. In the past few days, I'd come to think of Karl as a friend. Now that he was gone, I keenly felt his absence. "I'm sorry I never got to meet him."

Zeke nodded. "I'm sure he would have loved to meet you as well."

Logan cleared his throat. "What about the…" he pulled a package from the pack around his waist. It was wrapped in brown paper and tied with twine.

"Oh, yes, the treasure." Zeke took the box and handed it to me. "You earned this."

I took the parcel; it was lighter than I expected. "I feel like I've already received the treasure. This adventure, this time with my family." I looked at my parents and sister and my throat tightened. "It's been the real gift."

"Karl would have loved to hear that." Logan wiped his cheek, then set his face back to stoic mode. "Well, ya gonna open it or what?"

I ripped the brown paper to find a hand carved wooden box with the symbol for the US Navy burnished into the wood. "That belonged to my dad." Zeke took a step forward so that he could look at the box.

I turned the box over and admired the craftsmanship. "It's beautiful."

"There's something inside. Open it."

The hinges let out small creaks of protest as I opened the lid. The inside was covered in a deep blue velvet. Sitting in the middle was a metal clam shell shaped compact. It was covered in blue enamel and deep green stones. Gold filigree adorned the top, and the clasp was gold as well.

Zeke nodded toward the treasure. "Dad had a friend in Georgia that was a goldsmith. He did the filigree. The emeralds came from right here in North Carolina. Dad tried to tell me that the gold came from melted down coins from the Atocha, but I think that's just an old sailor's tale."

"Gold? Emeralds?" My grip tightened on the box. "I thought it was a proverbial treasure."

Zeke motioned toward the compact in my hand. "Dad also said that the greatest treasure lay inside. Why don't you open it up and see?"

I pressed the clasp, and the compact sprung open. When I raised it to my line of sight, I expected to see a pearl or another gemstone, but all I saw was my own reflection. "A mirror?" I said. "Is it from another shipwreck?"

Zeke took a step closer. I could smell his cologne, a mixture of musk and sea air. His breath tickled the back of my neck as he looked over my shoulder. I could see his reflection in the mirror beside mine. It was the first time I had noticed the way his green eyes had speckles of copper around the irises, and that a small dimple formed in his left cheek when he smiled. To my horror, I saw my reflection's cheeks turn pink.

Thankfully, Zeke didn't seem to notice my blushing. "There's nothing historic about the mirror. Dad always said that people seldom realize their own personal worth. He wanted whoever found the mirror to realize what a treasure they were." The dimple in his cheek deepened as his smile grew. "Dad was a bit dramatic like that."

I closed the compact, then spun on my heel. I handed the box to Zeke. "I can't keep this."

His smile faded. "Why not?"

"Your father obviously put a lot of love and care into this. I don't feel right keeping it. You're his son; you should have it."

Zeke put his hands on mine, curling my fingers over the clam-shaped box. "I appreciate that, but I have many things to remember him by. This is what he wanted. It would make him happy to know that somebody with your kindness found his treasure."

Suddenly a sound like wild deer came from the doorway. Brayden and Bentley burst into the room. "Aunt Timone, Daddy said you found the treasure. Is it true?" Brayden asked.

"Did it have gold doubloons?" Bentley squeezed between Zeke and me and grabbed my hand. "Awe, it's just a stupid jewelry box."

"Are there jewels inside?" Brayden hip-checked his brother out of the way.

I dropped to one knee so that I was on the same level as the twins. "Some things are more valuable than gold."

"Like platinum?" Bentley asked.

I touched him on the nose. "No, like memories."

Brayden threw his head back and let out a pathetic moan. "Are you going to start talking about feelings?"

Logan let out a belly laugh. Then he put a meaty hand on each of the twins' shoulders. "You boys want to see the parts of the museum that are closed to the public?"

Dad took a step forward, his eyes brighter than the twins'. "You can do that?"

Logan pointed to the logo on his shirt. "I can do anything I want."

Dad rubbed his palms together. "There are things I would love to see!"

"Retired Navy guy wants to see more nautical stuff. What a surprise?" Mom sighed.

As the rest of the family followed Logan, Zeke and I were left alone for the first time. Though the temperature hadn't changed, I noticed Zeke's forehead break out in a beaded sweat. "I'm sorry. My uncle is about as subtle as a sledgehammer."

"It's okay. I understand why he was upset. He wanted to be a part of the hunt for his brother's treasure."

"That's not what I meant." He motioned around the room, and I noticed that Zeke and I were totally alone.

"Oh," I felt my cheeks turn fuchsia.

"We can catch up with them." He rubbed the back of his neck. "Or there are some beautiful shells on the beach if you'd like to take a walk."

The adorable way his ears turned pink made me smile. I nodded. "I'd love to look for shells. Most of the ones where we are staying are broken when they wash up onto the shore."

Zeke gave me a sideways glance. "Just because they are broken doesn't mean they aren't still beautiful."

2

Driving East with My Daughters

"Stupid mosquitoes." My husband, Marcus, slapped his forearm. "Sure you don't want to take a few of them with you, Mary?"

I leaned against him, breathing in the woodsy must of his aftershave. "From what I've read, they have mosquitos in West Virginia, too. I really wish you could come with us."

He ran his fingers through my messy hair, his fingers catching on a snarl at the base of my neck. It was something that would have usually annoyed the daylights out of me, but in the wake of a two-week separation, I found it almost endearing. "I wish I could, babe. But the Miller account is due in nine days. Besides, I think this trip will be good for you and the girls. Hope is leaving for college in the fall, and Felicity will be behind her in just two years I think the three of you need this."

"Need what?" Hope, our lanky, raven-haired, fully made up, eighteen-year-old, walked through the front door and lowered herself down on the wicker couch.

"Female bonding." Marcus gave her a wink.

Felicity, our curvy, blond, dread-locked, sixteen-year-old, struggled onto the porch with an oversized suitcase rolling behind her. "Bonding is such a boomer word." She plopped down beside her sister.

"We aren't boomers." I shook my finger at her. "We are proud Gen X."

"Then why do you talk like boomers." Felicity rolled her eyes. "And why do we need to leave SO early? Am I going to get to drive on this trip? Are you sure you packed enough snacks? You know I don't like most restaurants."

"I'd like to arrive in one piece, so I say no to her driving." Hope nodded toward her sister.

Felicity scrunched up her face and glared at her sister. "You're such a b—"

"Felicity Dawn," I yelled.

Felicity turned to face me. "I was going to say bad sister."

I looked to Marcus for reinforcement, but all I got was a puckish smile. "See, they're already bonding."

I pressed my lips into a thin line and glared at him.

"Okay, so now may not be the best time for humor." He held up his hands defensively. His voice softened, and he kissed my temple. "But I honestly believe this time with the girls will be good for all three of you. No matter what you find in West Virginia, you'll be glad you took this trip."

I looked at our teen daughters who were now in a shoving match. "I hope you're right."

Though the idea of spending twenty-six plus hours in a car with two bickering teens caused my blood pressure to rise, it was the anxiety of what I would find waiting for me in Mount Storm, West Virginia that kept me up at night. You see, I wasn't heading to The Mountain State for its majestic vistas, I was on a quest to find information about from whence I had come, information about my birth parents.

I guess I need to give a little back story. My mom and dad, the people who raised me, were amazing parents. They never hid the fact that I'd been adopted as an infant, and for the longest time I was content. But as I entered the fourth decade of my life, I wondered about my biological parents, who they were, and why they had given me up.

My quest for answers soon became an obsession. Every free moment of my time was occupied with finding the truth. I didn't realize how much of an impact my search had on my family until New Year's Eve. A series of frustrations had sent Felicity spiraling into a meltdown. Once the screaming stopped, she sat at the foot of her bed and sobbed. "You never spend time with me anymore. You're always on your computer researching your other family. Why isn't this family enough?"

Her words were ice piercing my gut. I vowed to her, and to myself, that I'd give up the search.

Mom used to say, "If you want to make God laugh, make plans." Well, I'm sure the Big Guy is still chuckling over this. For six years, my research delivered dead ends and disappointment. Six days after I made a promise to let it go, I got an email from the confidential intermediary I'd hired to help me in my search. The subject line read: *I found your mother.*

My heart thudded as I opened the document, and my heart shattered when I read the first line. He had found my mother, and she was deceased. There was one silver lining though: he'd also found a woman who remembered my birth mother and knew my story. Verna, a seventy-two-year-old widow in Mount Storm, West Virginia, had lived on the farm beside my mother. She agreed to meet if I came to her.

Though I wanted to drive straight to the airport, jump on a plane, and fly to West Virginia, I'd made a promise to my daughter to give up the search, and I intended to keep my word. So, you can imagine my surprise when, in early June, the girls walked into my bedroom and announced, "Mom, we think you should meet Verna, and we want to come too."

That was how Hope, Felicity, and I found ourselves with our SUV packed on a Sunday morning ready to begin a 2,670-mile trek across the country.

I pulled myself out of Marcus embrace, making room for Felicity to give her dad a quick kiss goodbye. Then, she moved on to tearfully embracing our geriatric German Shepherd, Cedric. "Are you sure we can't take him with us? I'm going to miss him too much!" she wailed.

"You are such a drama queen," Hope admonished.

"I know you are, but what am I?" Felicity taunted in a snotty-tween voice.

Hope looked to her father. "Dad! Tell her to stop it!"

I pinched the bridge of my nose. "Both of you, in the car. Now!" I yelled so loud that Cedric ran behind Marcus' legs.

At least we were able to decide upon the seating arrangement. To start with, Felicity would drive, Hope would ride shotgun, and Mom would "relax" in the back. (Well, as much as a Mom can relax with her newly licensed sixteen-year-old driving)

We were two hours into the trip when Felicity grumbled, "Mom, my arms hurt, and my eyes are tired."

I looked up from my phone. "Hope, do you want to drive for a bit?"

Hope didn't reply. I looked closer and saw the white earbuds' cord snaking its way over her shoulder. I tapped her on the shoulder. "I asked you a question."

She ripped the earpiece from her ear. "What?" she snapped.

"Excuse me!" I returned her attitude. "Sorry to bother your ever important YouTube viewing, but I wanted to ask you something."

She turned back around. "I wasn't watching YouTube," she huffed. "If you must know, I was watching a Ted Talk by Bettina Bair."

I had no idea who that was, and I honestly didn't care. I was sick and tired of being her emotional punching bag. Over the past three months, my usually happy-go-lucky, eighteen-year-old daughter had become a sullen, moody stranger. I hoped it was just anxiety over leaving for Oregon State. My "Parents of Rising College Freshman" support group warned me that some kids pushed their parents away so that the initial separation wasn't so traumatic. Logically, it made sense, but it still hurt.

I adjusted my tone to "slightly less aggressive than Mary Poppins." "Who is Bettina Blair, honey?"

Hope seemed to accept my olive branch. "She's a computer science professor at Ohio State."

"Sounds fascinating."

Hope's tone softened. "You don't have to pretend. I know you hate it when Dad and I talk computer geek stuff."

"I don't hate it; I just don't understand it." I patted her shoulder. "You're going to do so many great things next year. I wish I had been smart enough to pursue a degree in computer programming."

Her shoulder tensed under my hand. But before I could ask why, Felicity slammed her palm on the steering wheel. "I said my arms hurt and my eyes are tired," she yelled. "Are one of you going to take over driving, or not?"

"Why are you always such a jerk?" Hope shook her head.

"I'm not a jerk! You're a jerk!"

"Yeah, because I'm the one who is screaming at people!"

Felicity's ears turned red. "Well, at least I'm not a… a…" She threw her hands in the air and let out a feral growl.

"Felicity, hands on the wheel!" I screamed.

Felicity straightened the SUV as it swerved onto the rumble strips. "You're such a drama queen."

I took a deep breath. "Just take the next exit, and I'll drive."

I sat back against the seat, rechecked my seat belt, and wondered how my two daughters could be so incredibly different from one another. Although Hope had recently become sullen, she'd always been predicable. Felicity was the epitome of the quote by Frida Kahlo, *"She's not fragile like a flower. She's fragile like a bomb."* Though I knew Felicity's determination, unique perspectives, and unquenchable curiosity would take her to brilliant places in life, I questioned if my sanity would be intact when she reached her destination.

After I took the wheel, things were peaceful. By peaceful, I mean each girl was glued to their phone while I listened to Radio Margaritaville on Sirius XM. I checked the estimated arrival time for our first stop, the Olive Garden in Elko, Nevada. Felicity was an extraordinarily picky eater. Food had to be exactly the right texture, temperature, and taste for her to tolerate it. Luckily, we had identified a handful of dishes made in chain restaurants that were a sure bet. Planning the family travel routes based upon the location of said restaurants was just natural for us.

After a calm meal filled with lazy conversation and unending bowls of pasta, I ordered a black coffee to-go. I drove until my eyes got too heavy in Wendover, Utah.

Early the next morning, we started off on the next leg of our adventure. As we headed east on interstate eighty, I was driving with Hope in the back and Felicity beside me. In our family, the driver sets the radio station. I had chosen *Us and Them*, a podcast that tried to bridge ideological gaps and find common ground. The moderator, Trey Kay, was a West Virginia native. It was what had originally drawn me to the program.

Ever since my C.I. told me my birth mother was from a small town in West Virginia, I found myself drawn to the state. I educated myself about the Mothman, the New River Gorge, the Greenbank Observatory, and the Greenbrier bunker. I even watched the WVU Mountaineers play basketball. I became obsessed with Jennifer Garner, Brad Paisley, and artist like Trey.

Trey was finishing his final thoughts about the opioid crisis in the Mountain state when Felicity jerked her earbuds from her ears.

"Mom," she shouted. "Look at this!" She thrust her phone under my nose.

I swatted her hand away. "Not right now."

Felicity's voice rose an octave. "Mom, this is important!"

"So is keeping us alive by not running off the road."

Felicity crossed her arms over her chest. "Fine, if you have more important things to worry about."

I bit back the sarcasm dancing on my tongue. "Is there a way you can tell me so that I don't have to take my eyes off the road?"

"I just took this test, and it says…." She studied her phone screen. "It says I'm autistic."

I made a sound like air being let out of a balloon. "You can't put any faith in those tests. My co-worker's son is autistic, and you two are nothing alike." I put my hand on her elbow. "Honey, you're a straight-A student. You're active in theater and band. Autistic kids don't do that type of stuff."

Felicity continued to stare at her phone. "This says autism is a spectrum, not a one-size-fits-all thing, that there used to be something called Asperger's Syndrome, but now it is all Autism."

"You don't—"

She threw her hands in the air. "I knew you wouldn't take this seriously."

When she got an idea in her brain, she would ruminate endlessly. I knew from experience it would be easier if I just played along. So, I took a deep breath. "What did this quiz say that makes you think you're autistic?"

"This article says that women and girls on the autism spectrum are often misdiagnosed with General Anxiety Disorder, Attention Deficit Hyperactivity Disorder, or Bi-Polar disorder."

I could no longer control my sarcasm. "I'm sure BuzzFeed is the shining example of mental health diagnosis."

Felicity looked at me sideways. "This article is from the National Institute of Health."

"The NIH?" I sat back in my seat, rightfully humbled.

"After I got the results from the original test, I started doing research on autism in girls." She tapped her phone to her chin. "Don't I have a 540 for ADHD?"

I remembered back to when Felicity was twelve. Her free-spirited ways, which in primary school were deemed cute and quirky, had grown problematic in middle school. Marcus and I took her to a child psychiatrist for evaluation. He diagnosed her with ADHD and anxiety. He had also mentioned that she was showing signs of bi-polar disorder but was too young for an official diagnosis.

Felicity tapped my upper arm. "Mom! Are you listening to me?"

"Yes, sorry. I was just…" I pinched the bridge of my nose. "Yes, you have a 504 at school to accommodate for your ADHD and anxiety."

"I've never fit in. What if," her voice quivered. "What if it isn't because I'm a weirdo; what if it's because my brain is different?"

The pain in her voice broke my heart. "Honey, you're not a weirdo. You're a bit eclectic, but that's just part of what makes you special." I took a deep breath. "Okay, what type of questions did the survey ask?"

She looked at her phone screen. "Are you hypersensitive to smells, textures, tastes, or sounds?"

I chewed my bottom lip. "Are those signs of autism?"

"Yes. It's called Sensory Processing Disorder. It has comorbidity with Autism." She continued to read from her screen. "Do you hyper focus on ideas? Do you have a vision of what should happen in your head and get very upset if things don't go as anticipated? Do you wish to be sociable but fail to form a bond with peers? Do you follow special routines and get very upset when things change? Do you ever invent idiosyncratic words and expressions? And…" The corners of her mouth turned up in a sly smile. "Have you been described as eclectic?"

Every single statement fit her, fit her perfectly. My brain swam as I searched to find the right words, but all I could mutter was, "I don't know what to say."

Her smile was gone, and her forehead creased in concentration. "What if all this time that I thought I was a bad person, a broken, freak who couldn't learn how to make friends… what if all this time, it wasn't my fault?"

Shame crashed down upon my chest like a tsunami. My daughter thought she was a broken freak, and I had no idea? Moms are supposed to know how their kids feel, be their champion. How could I have failed so miserably? I swallowed back the lump forming in my throat. "Honey. I didn't realize things were so hard for you."

"I didn't want to stress you out." Her voice was small.

There was so much I wanted to say, but I kept my thoughts to myself. Instead, I said, "Tell me more about your research."

She read to me from the NIH article, and like a mosaic slowly taking shape, the pieces fell into place. The hypersensitivity to light, sound, and food, the need to stick to a routine, the high-pitched squeals when she got angry, they all made sense. "I'm so sorry I didn't see the signs."

Felicity shrugged. "I just thought I was a difficult child, that I was constantly messing up. I've always wanted to be good."

Her words were a dagger in my heart. I grabbed her hand. "You are good. You're better than good. You're extraordinary!"

She looked at the article on her phone as if it was a map to the Holy Grail. "Mom, this explains so much."

We talked for almost two hours. It was the longest conversation we'd had in years. She told me about how difficult her sophomore year of high school had been, about the bullies, about the teachers who made snide comments about her idiosyncrasies.

I wanted to ask her so much. I wanted to know why she didn't tell me about the bullies, why she never confided in me about the snotty teachers, but I held my tongue. This was her time to talk, her story to tell. I took in every word as we drove through the state of Utah.

When I finally felt I had the right to speak, I asked, "What do you need from me?"

She chewed her bottom lip. "I don't really know."

I looked at this beautiful young creature next to me. She was so brave, so authentic, so amazing. I wiped a tear from my cheek. "When we get home, we can call Dr. Caldwell. He's been your pediatrician since you were born. I'm sure he can give us some direction."

Felicity nodded her head. "I like that idea." She put her hand on my elbow. "Thanks mama."

She hadn't called me "mama" since she was five. I didn't realize how much I missed the term of endearment. "Any time, baby girl," I whispered.

The rest of the day was uneventful compared to the morning. Hope and Felicity argued over where to eat, who would get to have a bed by themselves, and who was a better driver. Through it all, I couldn't take my eyes off Felicity. I often found myself on the verge of tears. I didn't want to cry because my daughter might be autistic. I wanted to cry because of my failure as a mother.

Her words replayed in my head: *I've always wanted to be good.* Did I make her feel like she wasn't good? When I reprimanded her for fidgeting too much in church, when I got frustrated with her for being inflexible, when I grounded her for arguing… Had I made her feel damaged?

Though we drove twelve hours that day, when I climbed into bed, my mind would not quiet. I stayed up until after midnight doing research on girls on the autism spectrum and how they are frequently misdiagnosed because they don't exhibit the "typical" autism traits. I read testimonies from other mothers. Though no two stories were exactly the same, I could see a piece of my precious daughter in each narrative. Before I finally drifted off, I made a vow to be a better mother.

~ ~ ~

By 7:15 the following morning, I had thoroughly broken my vow to be a better mother. My mind and body were exhausted, and my nerves were shot. Hope and Felicity were already screaming at each other. The squawking of teen girl voices, combined with my own raggedness, led to one heck of a mommy-temper-tantrum. I stood in the middle of the hotel room with my hands on my hips. "Would you two shut the hell up?!"

Both girls turned, their eyes as big as saucers. "Mom," Hope gasped. "What crawled up your—"

The look on my face was enough to stop her mid-sass.

Felicity, on the other hand, didn't pick up on the don't-mess-with-mama vibe. She laughed maniacally. "Yeah, Mom, what crawled up your butt?"

Heat surged from my abdomen to the top of my head. Hope slapped her hand over her ears and waited for the explosion. But I did not explode. Instead, I clenched my teeth and hissed. "When I get out of the shower, your bags better be packed and ready to go." Then I marched to the bathroom and stood under the scalding water until my body was as red as my temperament.

When I walked out of the bathroom, the girls were each deeply engrossed in their phone, and neither seemed to remember my tantrum. We loaded our bags into the car, and after a stop at Starbucks, we were on the road again.

For one small sliver of time, all screens were put away, and we listened to Spotify. John Denver had just finished crooning about *Country Roads* when Hope whispered, "Mom?"

The tone of her voice set me on edge. This sheepish style of talking didn't fit her personality. I tried to hide my anxiety. "What is it, sweetie?"

"There's something I need to talk to you about."

I remembered Felicity's revelation yesterday and immediately wondered, *What have I missed about Hope?* I swallowed hard and fought to keep my voice level. "You can tell me anything," I said a bit too sweetly.

Hope fiddled with the ruby pendant around her neck. "I just don't want you to be disappointed."

That statement didn't ease my anxiety. I kept my eyes straight ahead. "Sometimes the hardest part is just saying it. Why don't you get it out there so we can talk about it? No matter what you do, I'm always going to love you."

She furrowed her brows. "I haven't done anything."

"Then why are you worried I'd be disappointed?"

"What you find in West Virginia... What if you aren't happy with what you find?"

I breathed a sigh of relief and then felt guilty. I was worried she'd done something catastrophic, and she was worried about me. I leaned back in the driver's seat. "I don't know what to expect, so I don't know if I can be disappointed."

"What if you find things out about your birth parents that you wish you didn't know?"

"I've asked myself that same question one hundred times."

"People say not knowing is the worst, but I don't think so. Do you remember when Grandma started falling all the time and forgetting people's names. You said not knowing was the worst part, but when we found out..." she trailed off.

I shuddered at the memory. Three years ago, my mother went from doing half marathons and destroying us in *Jeopardy* to tripping up the stairs and not remembering her name. As we searched for answers, I thought nothing could be worse than the helplessness of not knowing. Then we got the diagnosis, Glioblastoma, an aggressive form of brain cancer. I quickly learned that there are things worse than not knowing.

I didn't realize Felicity had been listening until I heard a sniffle come from the back seat. "I really miss Grandma," she whispered.

Tears filled my eyes. "Me too, baby."

Hope looked out the window. "What if your birth mom was a horrible person?"

It was a question that had kept me awake many a night. What if my birth mother was a drug addict who tortured puppies for fun? What if the day she gave me away was the happiest day of her life? How would I feel if I found out I was a product of rape?

These fears tormented me, but I wouldn't let them torment my girls. So, I put on a brave face. "Whatever I find, I will have you two by my side. So, I know I can handle anything."

Felicity leaned forward and whispered. "Do you remember that episode of the X-Files that happened in West Virginia where the babies had tails? What if you had a tail when you were born?"

Felicity's off-the-wall question was the break in tension that we needed. All three of us broke out into gales of laughter. Tears blurred my vision, and I ran onto the rumble strips on the side of the highway. I jerked the SUV back into the appropriate lane, and the three of us continued to giggle until we stopped for lunch.

When we finally got our food at Chick Fil A, I said, "Talking about Grandma gave me an idea. What if, on the way home, we go a little out of the way and visit with Granddad. I'm sure he would love to see you guys."

After my mom passed away, Dad moved to Colorado. He'd found a nice retirement community where he had become friends with other widowers.

"I like the idea." Felicity mumbled as crumbs fell from her mouth.

"You are a pig!" Hope rolled her eyes.

Felicity swallowed, then began making oinking sounds in her sister's face.

"If you don't get out of my face, I am going to smack—"

"Nobody is smacking anybody." I rubbed my temples. "Just finish your food so we can get back on the road."

Felicity shoved a waffle fry into her mouth. "Granddad and Mr. Frank are roommates, right?"

I nodded.

"Why does Mr. Frank have a king-size bed and that enormous bedroom and Granddad has that small bedroom with a single bed?"

I choked on my frozen lemonade, and both girls turned their attention to me. While I coughed and sputtered, I tried to organize my thoughts.

Every family has its secrets, and mine was no exception. My adoptive parents were amazing people. They were wonderful parents, and they loved one another very much, but they were never in love with each other. Because my dad was closeted gay man.

When Dad came home from the Korean conflict, men were not allowed to love other men, so he did what he was supposed to do. He found a nice girl, bought a small house, and tried to start a family. When they couldn't have a child the traditional way, they adopted.

I had never intentionally hidden my father's sexuality from my girls, but I also didn't feel like discussing it in the middle of a fast-food restaurant. I was thinking of a way to change the subject when Hope leaned in close and whispered, "Are Mr. Frank and Granddad a couple?"

Felicity cocked her head to the side. "But he was married to Grandma."

"Let's think about this logically." Hope held up a finger. "One, Granddad's toothbrush is in Mr. Frank's bathroom." She held up a second finger. "Two, they go on lavish cruises together." She held up a third finger. "Grandma and Granddad had separate bedrooms."

"Grandma said that was because Granddad snored so bad."

Hope gave her sister an exaggerated eye roll. "Granddad stayed with us over Thanksgiving. Your room was right next to his. Did you hear him snore?"

Felicity's eyes got as round as the chicken sandwich in my hand. "So, Granddad is gay?" She crinkled her forehead. "I don't get it. He was married to a woman?"

Hope shrugged. "Maybe he's bi?"

"Can old people be bi-sexual?" Felicity asked.

Hope shuddered. "I don't like to think about old people having sex. Like Mom and Dad, that's just gross." She accented the point by making a gagging sound.

I leaned forward and hissed between my teeth, "Your father and I are NOT old."

"You're not exactly young, either." Felicity mumbled under her breath.

I wasn't sure what horrified me more, discussing my father's sex life or the fact that my child thought I was old and disgusting. Finally, I leaned forward and took each girl by the hand. "You two listen to me." I made sure I had their attention. "Granddad is allowed to live his own life. The only thing that matters to me is that he was a wonderful father and that he loves the two of you more than anything."

The corners of Hope's mouth turned down. "When I was studying psychology, I learned that they used to put people who were gay in mental institutions or prison."

"That is true." I nodded. "So, can you understand why Granddad might want to keep things like his romantic life secret and why we owe it to him to respect his privacy?"

Felicity reached across the table and grabbed my frozen lemonade. "Are there any other family secrets that we don't know about?" She took a sip. "Are we connected to the Illuminati? Did Grandma work at Area 51? Do we have a crazy ancestor who hid treasure in the Sierra Nevada Mountains?"

I shook my head. "No, no, and no."

A mischievous grin spread across Hope's face as she leaned forward. "Tell the truth. Felicity was raised by wolves, wasn't she?"

"That's not funny!" Felicity slapped her sister on the arm.

"Do not hit me!" Hope said through clenched teeth.

"You know I don't like it when you joke like that!" Felicity screamed.

To my horror, the dining room became pin-drop quiet, and every eye turned to us. Even the toddler who'd been kicking the seat behind me stopped kicking to gawk. I leaned forward and hissed between my teeth. "Throw your trash away and go to the car."

"But I'm not finished," Hope protested.

"Yes, you are!" I shoveled food, wrappers, and drinks onto my tray. "Now get to the car before I'm the one to make a scene."

The air in the SUV was thick with tension. Felicity drove while Hope sat in the passenger seat watching her phone. Soon my irritation wore off, and guilt took its place. It had been less than twelve hours since I made a promise to be a better mother, and I had failed... twice.

I was deep in the trenches of self-flagellation when exhaustion took over and I fell asleep. I slept until somewhere in Illinois, when I was jerked from my slumber by a frantic screech of "NO!" coming from the driver's seat.

My eyes flew open, and time slowed. Tires squealed, my body was thrust forward, and a kerthunk reverberated throughout the SUV.

Adrenaline snapped me back to reality as time resumed its normal speed. I took stock of my surroundings. We were sitting at a dead stop on interstate eighty. Felicity sat in the driver seat, white-knuckled and shaking.

"Felicity, get into the median!" I yelled. "Pull over."

Hope snapped, "Mom, stop yelling at her; she's freaked out enough."

I forced my voice to sound calm. "Sweetie, we can't be stopped on the interstate. You need to pull into the median."

Felicity edged her way onto the shoulder and put the Honda into park. She looked at her sister. "You were right. You said I was a horrible driver. I never should have asked to drive. I'm such a screw-up."

Hope had her hand on her sister's shoulder. "It could have happened just as easily to Mom or me."

I looked from Hope to Felicity and then back to Hope. "What actually happened?"

Felicity finally looked at me. Her chin trembled. "I… I… hit something. I think it was a deer."

"You think you hit a deer?" I repeated.

Gigantic tears ran down her cheeks as she nodded.

I unbuckled my seatbelt. "You two stay here. I'm going to check it out." I climbed from the backseat and investigated the damage.

It took considerable effort to not vomit. Underneath the SUV was a bloody pile of hair and bones that barely resembled a mammal.

Felicity rolled down the driver's side window. Tears dripped from her chin. "Is it dead?"

I stood far enough away that my feet wouldn't touch carcass but close enough to put my hand on her shoulder. "It didn't suffer."

"I killed it!" she wailed.

"It was an accident, sissy." Hope tried to comfort her.

"It's dead, and it's because of me!" Felicity buried her head in her hands and sobbed.

Hope was doing a great job of comforting her sister, so I decided to evaluate the damage. I did my best to avoid the gruesome sight while I inspected the SUV. The grill was cracked, and the front bumper was barely hanging on. Parts of the deer seemed to be embedded in the undercarriage.

Hope yelled from the passenger seat, "I called 911."

"Good thinking." I climbed into the backseat. "Can you hit the hazard lights?"

Felicity mumbled something unintelligible, and Hope continued to rub her back.

I reached forward to comfort my youngest, then pulled back. I wanted to tell her it would be okay, that we all make mistakes, but Hope was doing such a good job of being the comforting big sister.

Within five minutes, an Illinois state trooper pulled up behind the SUV. He walked to the driver's side of the Honda and looked at the bloody deer carcass. "I'd ask what happened here, but it looks pretty obvious."

At his remark, Felicity fell apart again.

I gritted my teeth. "Hello, Officer."

He glanced at Felicity, and then at me. "Are you the mom?"

"Yes, sir."

He motioned toward Felicity. "Is she okay?" His tone dripped with condescension.

I could tell from her sobs that she was teetering on the edge of no return. I wanted to yell at the officer, "No, she isn't okay. She is a girl who loves all animals and just killed an innocent deer, and your tone isn't helping." However, I also had very little interest in spending the night in an Illinois county jail. So, I said in my most-respectful tone, "Can you please help us find a towing service?"

While the officer arranged for a tow truck, I began searching for a hotel. I knew that even if the vehicle was in traveling condition, my daughter was not.

The tow truck driver gave us a lift to the closest Holiday Inn. While Hope checked us in, I went across the street to Chili's to grab dinner (and a margarita while I waited). By the time I made it back to the room, both girls were deeply invested in whatever was happening on their phone screens.

I tried to sound extra cheery as I laid the food out on the small table. "How ya doin', chicas? Hope you're hungry."

Felicity looked at Hope and then at me. "It's been a hard day; I'm going to take a long shower."

I grabbed the plasticware from the bag. "What about your food?"

She lowered her eyes. "I'll eat it when I get out." Then she scurried to the bathroom.

When the bathroom door closed, I looked at Hope. "Is she going to be okay?"

"Yep, she's fine." Hope answered a bit too quickly. "Have you found out anything about the SUV?"

"The body shop called while I was waiting for the food. The pilot isn't totaled, but there is a lot of damage. We'll have to leave it here and get a rental car for the rest of the trip. Hopefully, they'll have the work complete when we make our way back through."

"Exactly how much time are we going to spend in West Virginia?"

I shrugged. "I had planned on seven days, but I took a full month off work. Your orientation for Oregon State isn't until July 19, so we don't have to rush."

Hope lowered her chin, and a tear spilled onto her cheek. "There's something I need to tell you."

I reached out for her. "Hope, what is it?"

She wiped her cheek. "You know how you said that even though Granddad wasn't who we thought he was, it didn't matter. We would love him and respect his decisions?"

Thoughts raced through my head: *Oh my God, she's a lesbian. Be cool. Remember all of those coming out stories you watched on MTV in college? Don't act shocked. Let her know you love her no matter what. Should I hug her? No, let her initiate contact.*

I cleared my throat, but before I could speak, Hope blurted, "I'm not going to Oregon State in the fall."

So, that was definitely not what I had expected. I pressed my lips into a fine line while I devised a fresh course of action.

"Mom." Hope looked at me with pleading eyes. "Are you mad?"

"I'm definitely not mad, but I'm just taking a moment to process." I tilted my head to the side. "You've dreamed of going to Oregon State since you were five."

Hope shrugged. "Dreams change."

"Is this because you are scared of moving three hours away; it is completely normal to be—"

Hope leapt to her feed. "That isn't it!"

"Sorry." I held up my hands defensively. "You don't want to go to Oregon State, that's fine." I took a few deep breaths. "You can always stay home and attend Butte Community College. One of my old roommates is in the admissions department. I can call her and get your application started." I grabbed my phone from my back pocket. "I think I still have her number."

"Mom…"

I scrolled through my contacts. "You know, Hope. I think this may be a wise decision. Your father and I started a 529 for you when you were born, but we didn't get to put as much back as we would have liked to. We were afraid you'd have to take out loans."

"Mom..."

I started tapping out a text. "This may end up being a positive thing. If you can stay at home for two years and save on room and board, we can save that money for graduate school or a down payment on—"

"Mom!" Her yell echoed off the walls, making me drop my phone. I raised my eyes to look at her. A mixture of frustration and anxiety was painted on her face. "Mom, I'm not going to go to college, at all."

If Hope had told me that the sky was magenta, I could not have been more surprised. This is the girl who learned how to code in second grade. She was designing her own computer programs by ninth grade. She had already lined up internships for between her freshman and sophomore year. She was brilliant; she was driven; she was ...

"Mom, did you hear me?" She plopped down on the bed. "I don't want to go to college, at least not now."

I took her hand. "Is this why you have been so distant lately?"

She nodded. "I was afraid you'd be disappointed. Growing up it was never, *Are you going to college?* It was, *Where are you going to college? What are you going to major in?*"

"I didn't realize I made you feel like that." I felt defeated. In two days, I'd realized that I'd failed both of my daughters. That had to be some kind of Mom-screw-up-record. I swallowed back my hurt feelings. "So, what is it that you want to do?"

Hope took my hand. "I want to do a gap year volunteer program."

"A gap year?"

"Do you remember Mariana, my manager at Café Sequoia?"

I nodded, still trying to wrap my head around all of this.

Hope continued, "Mariana served in the Peace Corp when she graduated from college. She taught English in Thailand for two years, and she said it was the most rewarding time of her life."

I rubbed my eyes with the heels of my hand. "I'm confused. You want to teach?"

"I want to join the Peace Corp, but it's really competitive and requires a thirty-month commitment. So, I did research and found InterExchange. They offer a gap year program where I could teach English to students in Thailand, like Marianna did. It only cost between five to ten thousand dollars."

I held up my hands. "Wait, wait, wait. You have to pay to volunteer?"

"I have to pay for room and board while I volunteer." Hope took my hand. "Mom, I know this is a shock, but deep in my heart, I know this is what I want to do. I want to make a difference, leave a mark on the world."

I pushed myself onto my feet and walked to the other side of the room. "Have you talked to your father about this?

She shook her head. "Are you mad?"

I rushed back to the bed and took her hands in mine. "No, I'm not mad. It's just going to take me a little time to wrap my head around it, that's all."

"I've been emailing the company for a few weeks now. We can set up an online conference where you can ask all the questions you want." She sniffled. "You sure you aren't disappointed in me?"

I gently squeezed her hands. "How could I be disappointed that you want to make the world a better place?"

She exhaled. "You've always stressed the importance of getting an education and how important it is for a woman to be able to support herself."

"There's more than one way to get an education and support yourself." I pushed a strand of hair behind her ear. "If you want to take a gap year to volunteer, work, or try to decide what you want to study, your father and I will support that."

She sat up straight. "So, you're good with InterExchange?"

I held up a finger. "I didn't say that. Your father and I have to research this company."

I felt her deflate beside me.

I continued, "If it is safe, and reputable, and a good investment, then we can decide together what the next step will be."

She wiped a tear from her cheek and let out a weak laugh. "I guess that's a pretty good compromise."

As we hugged, Felicity walked out of the bathroom, a billow of steam following her. She looked at Hope. "So, how did she take it?"

"I'm right here," I tried to joke.

Hope smiled at me and then at her sister. "It's going to take some time for it to sink in, but I think she's going to be just fine."

That night, we sat in one bed and watched old episodes of *Dr. Who* on the BBC. We popped popcorn in the microwave and made virgin mimosas. As I watched my girls, a bit of melancholy tiptoed in. It seemed like just yesterday we were watching *Elmo's World* and talking about mermaids. But more than sadness, I felt pride. My girls were becoming such amazing, powerful, intelligent young women. Watching them grow was the greatest privilege in the world. This trip, even with all its revelations, fights, and roadkill, was such a gift.

Then I remembered the reason for this trip, to find out about my own mother. I couldn't help but wonder why she'd chosen to miss out on moments like this.

~ ~ ~

In the morning, we picked up the rental car, a maroon sedan that smelled like cigarette smoke, and continued our trip east. When we finally saw the sign on Interstate seventy that read *Welcome to West Virginia, Wild and Wonderful*, my heart leapt to my throat. In less than three hours, we would arrive at our condominium in Canaan, and in less than twenty-four hours, I would meet the woman who would tell me about my mother.

As soon as we arrived at the resort, I called my C.I. to double check the arrangements. He confirmed a noon meeting with Miss Verna Mitchell, at the Allegheny Mountain Top Public Library.

Anxiety kept me from resting. Though I wouldn't be meeting with Verna until noon, I was awake at five. I let the girls sleep in as I crept onto our deck and watched the sunrise over the Allegheny Front. After traveling through the Rockies, it was hard to call these lush mounds mountains. However, their beauty was impossible to deny. The mist rising from the valleys, the rhododendron in bloom, the blue ridges sloping this way and that. I understood why John Denver had called West Virginia almost heaven.

At approximately nine, the girls joined me on the deck. We watched bunny rabbits scurry back and forth as we had coffee and doughnuts. When it was finally time, we loaded into the sedan and made our way through meandering two-lane roads. Gigantic wind turbines spun lazily as we passed through their shadows. Finally, we saw a small green and white sign that read, *Mount Storm Unincorporated*.

Felicity leaned forward. "Mom, is this an actual town?"

I looked down at my phone; I was getting no bars. I pulled up the in-dash GPS. "This says we're in the right spot."

"Where are we meeting this Verna, again?" Hope asked.

"The Public Library. The directions I got from the C.I. say to head south on rural route forty-two and look for a brown brick building on the right."

Within minutes, we had arrived. The library was no bigger than a ranch style home. I parked between a rusty Chevy pickup and a red Ford Explorer, and then I froze. I mean, I literally could not move. All this time, years of searching, what if it was just another disappointment waiting to happen? What if this was like Mom's cancer, where the unknown was worse than the truth? What if Verna didn't really know my mom, and this was some ploy to exploit money from me? What if I'd dragged my girls across the country just so they could watch their mother's heart get shattered?

Felicity piped up from the back seat, interrupting my thoughts. "What if this is some devious plot, and a serial killer is waiting inside to chop us up and use one of those gigantic wind turbines to spray our remains all along the mountain top?"

Hope spun around. "What kind of messed-up, freaky thoughts happen inside that brain of yours?"

Giggles erupted from my mouth. The absurdity of Felicity's scenario combined with a lack of sleep and excess of stress to send me over the edge. Before I knew it, my giggles had evolved to full-blown belly laughs. My eyes watered, and snot ran from my nose. My daughters stared at me, open mouthed.

"Mom, are you okay?" Hope put her hand on my elbow.

"I think she's losing it," Felicity whispered.

I wiped my face, then turned to look at Felicity and Hope. "You two are the best travel partners ever. Thank you for doing this with me."

The girls exchanged looks that told me that they definitely believed I had lost it.

I put a hand on each of their shoulders. "I appreciate you traveling with me all this way, but this next part, I need to do on my own."

"What?" Felicity gasped. "We don't get to meet Verna?"

"You can meet her, but I want to speak with her by myself for a few minutes."

Hope chewed her bottom lip. "We understand." She looked pointedly at Felicity. "Don't we, Sissy?"

Felicity crossed her arms over her chest. "I guess so," she mumbled.

I said, "If in twenty minutes I haven't returned to the car, come find me inside."

~ ~ ~

My stomach felt like a den of writhing snakes as I walked through those white doors. What I wouldn't give for one of Felicity's off-the-wall comments to distract me, but like I told the girls in the car, I had to do this alone. If I did find out something horrific, it was my job to protect my daughters.

I scanned the room and saw a petite woman in a long skirt sitting in a comfy-looking burgundy chair. Her gray hair was piled high on her head, and her hands shook as she turned the pages of the magazine she was reading.

I pushed back my shoulders and walked toward the sitting area. "Excuse me, are you Verna?"

The woman's eyes met mine. She sucked in a quick breath, then lifted her hand to her mouth. "You have her eyes."

I forced my breathing to remain steady, but my body broke out with goosebumps. I wanted to speak, but I didn't trust my voice.

Verna stood and took my hand. "I can see parts of your daddy in you too."

"You knew my father?" Every greeting I'd rehearsed, every question I wanted to ask, went out the window. Instead, I collapsed into the chair across from her. "I assumed she was young and alone, and that is why she gave me up." To grow up knowing that one parent didn't want you was one thing; to know that both gave you away was crushing. Tears welled up in my eyes, and a gigantic sob escaped from my chest. "So, he didn't want me either."

Verna gripped my wrist with surprising strength. She sat in the seat across from me and pulled me to her, until her face was less than an inch from mine. The wrinkles around her steel-gray eyes were sad yet resolute. "You listen here. Your parents loved you more than you'll ever know. They did what they thought was best for you, what they was told was best for you. Never think for a moment that you were not wanted."

"What they were told was best for me?"

Her eyes softened. "It's a long, sad story."

I blinked back tears. "That's why I'm here. I need to know the story."

Verna's shoulders slumped, as if she was suddenly exhausted. When she began to speak, her voice sounded far off. "Your mother was a sweet girl. She was a dear friend, but your mother was," she paused to find the right word, "special."

"Special? How do you mean?"

Verna nodded. "In those days we called girls like her slow or strange."

"My mother had an intellectual disability?" I choked out.

"It was the strangest thing. Sometimes she would chatter away about the most obscure thing, but when you would ask her a question, it was like she was a mute. She would do this thing where she flapped her hands and spun in circles, even when she was a grown woman."

And another piece of Felicity's puzzle fell into place. I filed that piece of information for later, then asked, "Was she happy?"

"I believe she was. Back in those days, we didn't have special education and all the things we have now. So, her parents kept her at home and didn't send her to school beyond the sixth grade. It was too much for her to sit still for so long, you see. But your grandmother, Eva, taught her how to read and write." Deep wrinkles formed in the corner of Verna's mouth when she smiled. "Eva always said that your momma had a brilliant brain; she just didn't know how to tell everybody all the things she knew."

"I know somebody very similar."

"Then you know how special they are."

I sat back in my chair. "The paperwork that I found said she was twenty when I was born."

Verna thought for a moment. "I reckon that's about right. Even at that age, your grandparents didn't believe she could take care of—"

"Arleta. My mother's name was Arleta, can you please use her name? I know it seems like such a small thing, but all my life she has been this nameless entity. I want to call her by her name."

Verna nodded. "Arleta's parents didn't think she could take care of you, and they were too old to raise a baby, so you were put up for adoption." Tears filled Verna's eyes as she leaned closer. "Were your parents good to you? Were they good people?"

I took her hand. "They were the best parents in the world."

"That's the thing Arleta worried about the most. She was heartbroken that she couldn't raise you, but I believe if she'd known you were being raised by good people, it would have given her peace."

"I wish somebody could have told her."

Verna squeezed my hand. "She and your daddy talked about you a lot. They never forgot about their baby, Mary."

"Do you know why my father's name is not on my birth certificate?"

Verna sat back in her chair. "I'm afraid I don't, but I suspect it's because Henry was a bit special in his own way. He was a sweet man, and he loved your mama, but he was slow, a bit of a child himself."

Too much was coming at me. I held up my hands in a halting motion. "So let me get this straight, my mother and father were both intellectually delayed. I was conceived, and my grandparents made them put me up for adoption? Nobody even gave them the chance to try?" My eyes burned as I remembered the all-consuming sense of love and attachment I felt when my girls were born. If someone had forced me to give them away. The pain my mother must have felt... And my father, did they even understand what was happening? A heavy weight bore down on my chest. My lungs fought for oxygen, but short, gasping breaths was all my body would allow. I doubled over as the pain in my chest became unbearable, and the corners of my vision started to blur.

Before I knew what was happening, Verna was kneeling beside my chair. "Mary," she put her palms on my cheeks. They were soft and cool against my flushed skin. "Mary, you are safe. You are in a library in Mount Storm, West Virginia. My name is Verna Mitchell. You drove from Oregon to meet me." She rubbed her thumbs over my cheekbones. "Take small breaths. I'm right here beside you. In... out.... Good, just like that."

I put my head between my knees and concentrated on breathing in time with her words. Finally, my pulse stopped racing, and I raised my head. I looked at the woman kneeling before me. Her jaw was set in determination, but her eyes were full of compassion.

She took my hands in hers. "Have you ever had a panic attack before?"

"Yes, but not for a long time."

"I know it's been a lot to take in. Just keep taking cleansing breaths. Good. Like that." She kept her hands around my own. "My Johnny had attacks like that when he came back from Korea. The only thing that got him through was me talking to him in that voice."

I squeezed her hands. "My dad, my adopted dad, served in Korea, too."

"Did he have the screaming dreams?"

"If he did, he hid them well. I never noticed them."

"It's a parent's job to hide their pain from their children."

The word "parent" reminded me of why I'd come to find information about my birth parents. I sat up straight. "I know my mom passed away when she was forty, but what about my father? What happened to Henry?"

"He's in a nursing home in Petersburg. It's about half an hour from here."

"He's still alive!" I yelled.

The librarian shot me a reproachful look. I lowered my voice. "My father is still alive."

Verna's mouth drooped at the corners. "He is, but…"

"But what?"

She took a deep breath. "People who are… people like your father, are more susceptible to dementia. He's been pretty far gone for a while now."

A cold pain rippled through my chest. "Oh, I see."

"They take good care of him. Last time I saw him, he was in his own little world, but he was happy there."

"How do you think he'd react to meeting me?"

She shook her head. "I don't know. He may not understand who you are. His nurses could give you better guidance than I could. I can give you the number of the facility if you'd like to call."

I imagined walking into a room and seeing a stranger, my father, sitting in a bed. Would I cry? Would I smile? If I did cry, how would it affect him? Would he think I was a stranger? Would he recognize me as his daughter? If he remembered, would seeing me remind him of the most painful thing he had ever lived through?

Verna patted my hand. "You don't have to decide right now. Think on it and then make up your mind later."

"Thank you, Verna. Thank you for everything. All my life I felt like a puzzle who was missing its final piece." I started to say more, but a motion over Verna's right shoulder caught my attention. I looked up to see my daughters walking through the doors of the library. Hope looked timid, but Felicity looked as if she was ready to wrestle a bear.

I looked at my watch and laughed. I'd told them to give me twenty minutes, and exactly twenty-one minutes had passed.

I looked back to Verna. "My girls traveled with me from Oregon. I told them to wait in the car, but they didn't listen."

Verna turned to look at the two strange teenagers standing at the door. She smiled widely. "The younger one looks a lot like your daddy."

I buried that sweet sentiment deep in my heart. "They would love to meet you. Would you be willing to talk to them, tell them stories about my mother and father?"

"I would be delighted."

When my girls joined us, Verna greeted them with grandmother-worthy hugs. We sat around the conference table as I explained about my parents' intellectual difficulties and the reasons behind me being put up for adoption. Felicity asked question after question, and Verna answered each and every one with patience. All the while, Hope held my hand and closely watched my reactions.

After about twenty minutes, I asked Verna. "I hope it doesn't sound morose, but I want to visit my mother's grave. Can you take me to where she is buried?"

"I'd be happy to."

"We get to come too, right?" Felicity asked.

Verna said, "It's in an old family cemetery at the top of Lillian's Ridge. Your car may not make it up there. We should probably take my Explorer."

~ ~ ~

As we bumped along the rutted, dirt road, Hope became more introverted, while Felicity continued with her rapid-fire question assault.

"Why are there so many windmills along the highway? Do you get free electricity? Did my grandmother have a horse? Is this place called Mount Storm because it is on top of the mountain, and it storms a lot? Do you remember the day Mom was born?"

As Verna drove, she was the epitome of patience.

When we finally turned from the main dirt road onto what Verna called a two-track, I was very glad I didn't try to bring my rental sedan. We drove a few hundred yards, then arrived at a small plot of land surrounded by a cast iron fence.

Verna put the SUV into park. "I figured you would want to visit your mom, so I had some men from the church brush hog the cemetery." She motioned to the surrounding area. "The rest of this is usually made into hay, but then we had such a dry spring that they didn't even get a second cut. The Klines decided to just use it for pasture later."

I nodded like I knew what she was talking about as I climbed from the passenger seat. The smell of freshly cut grass filled my nostrils. I turned a full three-hundred-sixty degrees to take in the view. The lush hardwoods mixed with the deep pines to form a patchwork of green. The manicured fields in the valleys, the occasional white farmhouse in a clearing created a scene that was simply breathtaking.

Hope stood at my side. "What a peaceful spot for a final resting place."

"It certainly is." I turned to the right and saw the gray granite stones. My nerve faltered.

When I received the original report from my C.I. that he had found my mother and that she had passed, a fissure formed in my heart. When I heard Verna talk about her battle with Ovarian Cancer and her death, the crack deepened. If I saw her grave, stood at the place where her body lay, would my poor heart completely shatter?

Verna put her hand on my shoulder. "I'm going to go say hi to my Uncle Billy, you take your time."

"Does Billy live close by?" Felicity asked.

Verna chuckled. "He's buried at the top of the hill."

"Oh, I'm sorry. I misunderstood. When you said you were going to say hello, I assumed the person was still alive," Felicity overexplained.

"No need to apologize, my dear." Verna let out a soft chuckle then put her hand on each girl's elbow. "Why don't you two come with me and give your momma a moment?"

After the girls and Verna started up the hill, I stood beside the SUV for ten minutes trying to muster the courage to follow. The woman who gave me life, the woman who gave me up so that I could have a better life, lay less than a hundred yards from where I stood. I owed it to her to pay my respects, to say thank you.

This is all I'd dreamed of doing these past few weeks, but now that I had my chance, my feet felt as if they were encased in cement. I willed myself to take a step, and then another, and then another. Finally, I was inside the graveyard, where I saw Verna and my girls standing beside a small stone. The top had been carved into the shape of a lamb.

My feet continued without my permission, as my peripheral vision blurred. When I was two feet away, I collapsed to my knees to read the inscription:

Arleta Francine Kesner

1950-1990

Daughter, Friend, Child of God

I reached out and wiped the pale green lichen from the lamb's coat as words tumbled from my mouth. Tears and snot dripped down my face as I told my mother about the wonderful people who had raised me. I thanked her for giving me life and for watching over me. I told her about my husband, Marcus, and I told her how much I loved her.

After a few minutes, Felicity and Hope knelt on either side of me. I took their hands in mine, and each placed their free hand on the lamb. A soft electricity flowed between us, from mother to daughter and for the first time in my life, daughter to mother. We sat at her grave until pins and needles began to prick my legs. When I felt as if I'd said everything I'd come to say, I kissed the lamb atop the gravestone and promised to return.

As we climbed back into Verna's SUV, I asked, "Is there a local person who can make amendments to grave markers?"

"I reckon Shaffers could do it. That's the funeral home in Petersburg." Verna scrunched her eyebrows. "May I ask why?"

"There's something missing from the inscription." I held my chin high. "It says *Daughter, Friend, Child of God*."

"That is the inscription I decided upon when she was buried."

I swallowed. "I want to add: *Beloved Mother*."

Verna put her hand on my knee. "I shall see that it gets done.

3

Auntie P, The Matchmaker

July 2020

Finding your soulmate is hard.

Finding your soulmate when you are over forty is *double* hard.

Finding your soulmate when you are over forty and in the middle of a global pandemic is dang-near *impossible*.

As a certified public accountant, I know numbers – my whole life is numbers - so I fully understand the theoretical probability of dang-near impossible. It's like one in a kagillion.

But still, one.

I didn't hate being single. I'd gone through enough deadbeats, overgrown toddlers, and mommy-issues-havers to last a lifetime. I was completely content to be a corporate CPA and dog mom living in solitude, or so I thought.

Then in March of 2020, the Coronavirus forced the world to shut down. Turns out, puppy playdates, cocktails with friends, and traveling the country on your own doesn't count as solitude. Locked inside your home with only Zoom teleconferences, social media, and phone calls to your mother was the true meaning of solitude. And I did not like solitude.

By early July, I was stir-crazy. I missed my girlfriends. I missed my co-workers. Hell, I even missed the annoying barista at Starbucks who couldn't spell my name. The only thing that kept me sane was my daily call to my mother.

She always picked up after the first ring. "Jada Michelle, so nice to finally hear from you." It was our running joke. I'd called my mom every day since I left for Howard University the late nineties.

"Nice to talk to you too, Mom. How's the weather there?" Every conversation started with the weather. If it had rained, Mom would tell me how much she had collected in her rain gauge and how much each of her neighbors had collected in theirs. If it was sunny, she would tell me the high and low temp for the day. Then, the conversation went to hometown gossip: who was getting married, who was getting divorced. Recently, the gossip sessions ended with who had gotten the virus, who had recovered, and who had not.

Our conversations had a lazy cadence to them, and that predictability brought me comfort in these unprecedented times. So when, out of the blue, Mom dropped, "Jada, you need to find yourself a good man," I was shaken—not only by the subject matter, but also by the dramatic change in routine.

"I… ah… um…" was my only reply.

She continued, "Now, I know that dating during this pandemic is hard. You can't go out and see people or meet at restaurants, but that may be a good thing. If you go onto one of those dating sites you could chat with somebody for a while. Ya' know, see if they are worth your time before you ever see them face to face." Mom laughed. "I was talking to Ann Marie the other day. Her daughter, Zena, met this nice fella on this site called Black People Meet."

"Uh huh," I responded, not missing the fact that she name-dropped the website.

Mom continued. "Zena and this fella talked for almost six weeks before they met up at a park. Ann Marie said he's as ugly as a rhino's rear end, but that Zena and he had such a connection, she didn't mind his bad looks."

I pinched the bridge of my nose. "I'll think about it, Mom."

"You do that." She paused. "Sweetie, Your Aunt Ruby is on the other line. I'll talk to you tomorrow. Love you."

"Love you too, Mom," I said, then clicked off the phone.

I grabbed another cup of coffee and headed to my spare bedroom turned office. Zeus, my loyal rescue mutt, followed me. He slept on the bed as I returned the emails, filled out spreadsheets, and got sucked into arguments between strangers on social media.

After about an hour, I felt a paw on my lap. The moment I showed Zeus the slightest bit of attention, he rolled onto his back and looked at me as if to say, "This belly ain't gonna scratch itself."

"You're the definition of pathetic," I chided as I bent down to scratch his ribs. "My mom wants me to try online dating. Can you believe that?"

Zeus gave me a sympathetic look.

"If I do make an online profile, it will be very clear that we are a packaged deal. Love me, love my mutt. Does that make you happy? Because if they don't like my puppy dog, they can just walk—"

The moment the w-word was out of my mouth, Zeus made a crazy twisting motion that catapulted him from flat on his back to standing on all fours. The top of his skull connected with the soft cartilage of my nose. My hands flew to my face.

"Dude, not cool." I glared at him through teary eyes.

Zeus whimpered, and I lowered my hands. A pair of remorseful puppy eyes was staring back at me. My stone-cold heart melted. "You're just lucky you're cute." I got to my feet. "Let's go take that walk."

The definition of walk had changed a lot since March. I did my best to follow the CDC guidelines. If I was in public, I wore a mask. When I was outside, I kept six feet between me and a stranger… unless… unless a furry creature was involved.

Three weeks into the lockdown, I took Zeus to the park. I saw a little girl with a kitten, and all my common sense flew straight out the window. Before I could stop myself, I was up in that little girl's personal space petting that cute baby cat. After a well-deserved reproach from the girl's mom, I made a vow to walk Zeus around my neighborhood instead of the park. I flat out could not trust myself when it came to fur babies.

The upside was that it gave me a chance to get to know my neighbors. There was Rudy, a yellow lab who needed to go on a diet, Harold, teacup with Yorkie with Napoleon syndrome, and Carly, the wiener dog with a sweet smile. Carly lived with the Allen family and my new favorite human Auntie P

Aunty P, whose real name was Petunia Burns, was short, wobbly, and full of fire. Her white curly hair was always perfectly quaffed, even on the most humid of days. Deep lines surrounded her intelligent brown eyes, and her mouth was set in a constant smirk. From her first sarcastic comment, we became instant friends.

On that warm July morning, I saw Auntie P was sitting on the front porch. So, I tugged Zeus' leash in that direction.

"Well, hello, girlie," Auntie P called as I approached. "How's your pup today?"

I dropped Zeus' leash and allowed him to run onto the porch. He went straight to Aunty P and put his head in her lap. "Aren't you an attention monger?" She rubbed his ears, then he was off to find Carly.

I settled onto the bottom step, ready to tell Aunty P about the bizarre recommendation from my mom, when an unfamiliar baritone voice came from the side yard. "Well, hello, fella. You want a belly rub?"

I pushed myself to my feet and peered into the side yard. A man with rich, dark hair, dirty blue jeans, and stained t-shirt was on his knees scratching Zeus' belly. "That dog is definitely an attention monger," I muttered. I cupped my hands around my mouth. "Zeus, leave that poor man alone."

The man pushed himself to his feet. "Now look there, you got us both in trouble." There was a kindness in his baritone voice. As Zeus trotted back to my side, the man followed him with his eyes- brilliant sapphire blue eyes. "Your dog's beautiful. Is he a Shepherd Husky mix?"

Beautiful, that word was dancing on my lips. I looked away while I still had the ability to speak. "He is, but Auntie P says he's one hundred precent attention hound."

"Attention hound is my favorite breed. He reminds me of my Lacy. She was an Akita mix, but she had the same sweet personality as your boy." A hint of sadness colored his voice. "I lost her last spring to cancer."

"I'm so sorry." I looked back at him.

"She had a good long life, but I miss having a dog around." He crossed the yard in three long strides, stuck out his hand, then retracted it. "I keep forgetting about all of this social distancing stuff. I'm Gary, by the way."

"It's taking a lot of getting used to, that's for sure. I'm Jada," I pointed to my mutt, "and this is Zeus."

"Well, thank you for letting me play with your sweet boy." Gary looked at his watch. "I should get back to work. Nice meeting you, both."

I turned and walked back toward the porch. Aunt P had been watching the entire scene while her great-nieces set glasses of lemonade on the table.

"Hi, Miss Jada," Chanta said. "Nice of you to stop by."

"Hey, Chanta, how're you doing today?"

She shrugged. "Bored, like the day before, and the day before that. I can't wait for this stupid virus to go away. I made some lemonade for you and Auntie P." She handed me a glass.

"Well, aren't you just the sweetest thing?" I took a sip. "Mm Mm! Chanta this is amazing. It's just the right ratio of sugar to sour. You could bottle this!"

Chanta gave a wide grin, then disappeared back inside.

Aunty P took a long drink, then smacked her lips. "You're right. That ain't half bad." She sat her glass on the wicker table. "Sounded like Gary liked your dog an awful lot."

"Everybody loves Zeus." I tilted my head to the side. "Were you eavesdropping on us?"

She ignored my question. "You know, he's single."

I rolled my eyes. "Have you been talking to my mom? She was just on me today about how now would be a good time to find a man. She even wanted me to fill out one of those online dating apps. I mean, what if I don't want to find a man?"

Auntie P's lips formed a perfect "O." "Well, that would be okay with me. I know some of my generation are hung up on that type of thing, but if you are into women—"

I laughed so hard I spat out my drink. "N-N-No," I sputtered. "I like men, but I just haven't had a lot of luck in that area. Sometimes I wonder if happily ever after isn't for me."

"First of all, you have to forget all of that happily ever after manure. I swear Disney and this princess, fairy tale stuff has ruined an entire generation for thinking that is what love looks like. Prince Charming doesn't exist. Find an equal, a best friend, a partner in crime. You know, when I met my Malcolm, we…"

She talked for over an hour, and I hung on every word. Even the stories she'd told me ten times before, like how she and Malcolm were heartbroken when they realized she was barren, or about how they marched in Alabama with Dr. Martin Luther King Jr, captivated me. Aunty P was a living history book, and I soaked up each syllable of knowledge.

After an hour, I could tell she was getting tired. I pushed myself to my feet. "I should get going. It was wonderful talking to you. Same place tomorrow?"

Deep lines formed around her eyes as she smiled. "Same place tomorrow."

Auntie P made her way inside, while I made my way around back where Zeus was lying under a shade tree with Carly. I showed him the leash, and he lumbered toward me.

Gary was hard at work using a pickaxe to loosen the soil. I studied him from a distance. Every time he swung the ax, his white t-shirt stretched across his wide shoulders. I admired his narrow waist and muscular thighs. I bent down and whispered in Zeus' ear, "Now that's a nice view."

When I got home, I had a passive aggressive email from my supervisor waiting on me: *The meeting with Capaldi, Tennant, and Smith has been moved up. We need the reports by 8am tomorrow, good thing you don't have kids to take care of and can dedicate yourself to this.*

I felt the heat creep up my neck. He NEVER would have made that comment to a man. My fingers flew over the keyboard as I typed a reply: *Dear misogynistic, pompous ass hat…*

Zeus put a paw on my lap.

"What? He was really out of line."

He nudged my hand.

"Fine, I'll erase it." I scratched his chin. "But he really is a pompous, misogynistic ass hat."

Zeus sat at my feet and watched as I typed a more professional reply. Then, I closed my email and pulled up the spreadsheet. At eight o'clock that night, I finally pushed myself away from my desk.

~ ~ ~

Tuesday morning, I put on a professional blouse and sticky sweet smile to present the data to the company VP via Zoom meeting. When the meeting ended at noon, my eyes and patience had had enough. Zeus was tearing through the house like a maniac, and I decided we both needed some exercise.

To my disappointment, when we walked past the Allen's house, Aunty P wasn't on the front porch. Zeus saw Carly digging in the flower bed and tugged at the leash. The Allens and I had an agreement, if one was walking past the other's house and the dog being walked wanted to play with the dog at home, the walker of the dog had permission to come into the yard and have a puppy playdate.

I let Zeus off leash. He and Carly ran into the back yard to play. I followed to supervise and was pleasantly surprised when I saw Gary sitting under the shade tree eating a sandwich.

He waved, and I walked to the tree. I sat an appropriate distance away. "How's the deck coming along?" I asked.

Gary rolled his eyes. "Well, the deck is now going to be a patio, with a sunken fire pit and built-in seating."

"When did all of that change?"

"When Kimberly got home last evening. I guess Titus wanted something simple, but Kimberly had something else in mind." He smirked. "Guess who won."

I laughed. "Well, I guess that's good for you. Bigger project, bigger price tag."

"Any other summer, it would have been great. But this summer, with people working from home, everybody is wanting to tackle that backyard project they've been putting off. I set aside two weeks to complete this, hoping it would be an easy two weeks. Now, I'll be getting everything done just under the wire."

"Are you doing it all on your own?"

Gary nodded. "I own my own business. Sometimes I'll hire a high school kid who needs the extra money, but I'm mostly a one-man team."

"So, the pandemic has been good for business?"

The mention of money and business seemed to make him uncomfortable. "Something like that." He took a drink from his thermos then wiped his mouth. "What is it that you do?"

"I'm an accountant. I work for a large firm in Northern Virginia."

He looked away from me. "Big-time money and big-time clients?"

"Something like that." I hoped by repeating his phrase it would ease his discomfort, but he continued to stare into the middle distance. I thought a change of topic may lighten the mood. "My commute has gone from sixty minutes to sixty seconds, so that's a plus."

The corners of his mouth tipped downward. "Glad there's been an upside for you."

I couldn't identify the tone in his voice: annoyance, sarcasm, resentment? He pushed himself to his feet. "It was nice chatting with you again, Jada, but I gotta get back to work." Without another word, he strode back to the worksite.

I sat for a moment, utterly dumbfounded. The conversation had started out friendly, then the tone completely changed. I replayed the conversation, trying to pinpoint the moment when things became awkward, but I couldn't think of a single thing I'd said wrong. Finally, I pushed myself to my feet and made my way back to the front porch.

Aunty P was sitting in the rocking chair. "What did you and Gary talk about?"

I put my hands on my hips. "You have got to stop spying on me."

She peered at me over her wire rimmed glasses. "It's not spying if it is happening in your own backyard."

I took my normal spot on the bottom step and changed the subject. "Sounds like Kimberly and Titus have different opinions about the backyard."

Aunty P clucked her tongue. "That niece of mine…" We talked for a good hour before I had to head back to work.

~ ~ ~

As monotonous as the weekdays were in quarantine, the weekends were worse: no meetings, no conference calls, no distractions from the isolation. Aunty P was feeling a little under the weather, so there was no stopping by for a visit. My daily conversation with my mom was the only distraction. I considered mentioning Gary to her, but I knew it would only lead to a slew of questions, questions I didn't have the answer to.

Monday morning, I got a text from Aunty P saying she was feeling better and inviting me to lunch on the front porch. Unfortunately, knowing I had a fun lunch partner made the morning meetings tick by ever slower. When I finally logged off the last Zoom meeting, I desperately needed good company. So, I hitched up Zeus and made our way down the block.

To my delight, Aunty P was sitting on the front porch. She smiled as I approached the porch. "How's my favorite accountant today?"

"Full of coffee and still tired. I swear, I didn't realize doing nothing all weekend could be so exhausting." I sat on the top step. "I did watch some good TV this weekend, though."

"They don't make TV like they used to," Aunty P tutted. "*The Jeffersons, Andy Griffith, All in the Family.* I swear, *The Cosby Show* was the last decent TV program."

A voice came from behind me. "Am I interrupting anything?"

I turned to see Gary standing on the walkway. He had a brown paper bag and a thermos in hand. Though I didn't understand why, I felt irritation prickle up the back of my neck. Perhaps it was how awkward things had ended last time we talked. Maybe it was that he was infringing upon MY Aunty P time.

Aunty P motioned to three glasses of lemonade on the side table. "I had Chanta make a fresh batch this morning. Why don't you sit a spell?"

Then I realized what felt so strange about Gary appearing; this was a set up. Aunty P was matchmaking.

Gary shuffled from one foot to the other. "Are you sure? I don't want to be a third wheel."

Aunty P made a dismissive motion with her hand. "I invited you to have your lunch with me, didn't I?"

I closed my eyes and shook my head. This was definitely a set up. When I opened my eyes, Gary was looking at me apprehensively. Did he interpret my head shaking as me not wanting him here? I put an overly bright smile on my face. "Why don't I move to the other side of the porch, and you can sit here on the steps. That way we can keep our distance." I grabbed my lemonade and made my way to my spot.

Gary took his glass as well. "How are the Chanta and Cierra handling the isolation? I can't imagine being a teenager and being on lockdown like this."

"Well, it was going fine. They had their noses in their darn phones all the time, but we were managing until last night. Little Miss Cierra snuck out to visit a bunch of her friends. Her parents grounded her, but how can you ground a teenager when they're in lockdown? So, they took away her phone! Now, she's being a royal pain in the you-know-what."

"Please tell me it was outside!" Gary exclaimed. "Doesn't she realize how serious this is? Every major health organization is saying to limit inside gatherings."

Aunty P made a dismissive motion. "She's seventeen. She thinks she's invincible." She put her hand to her mouth. "Ya' know, I probably should have mentioned Cierra's little excursion before I invited you to lunch. Stupid old brain," she tapped her temple with her forefinger, "doesn't think through things sometimes."

"You should be fine." Gary shook his head. "Outside gatherings are not as dangerous as inside. It's the recycled air that poses the biggest threat."

"Would it make you feel better if I wore a mask?" I asked.

Aunty P shook her head. "No need for that, but perhaps I should go inside to keep from sharing my germs with you two." She pushed herself onto her feet. "Why don't we do this again, same time tomorrow?"

Before we could object, Aunty P had opened the screen door and slid inside.

I looked at Gary, who still looked angry. "I can't believe that girl would be so irresponsible. Her eighty-five-year-old aunt is living with her! If she brings that virus home... does she realize?"

I looked at the screen door and then back to Gary. "How much do you want to bet it's just a story?"

Gary's eyebrows formed a deep V. "Just a story? Do you think this entire pandemic is made up?"

I crossed my arms over my chest and gave him a good once over. "No! I believe the science!" I leaned back. "I was saying I think what Aunty P told us about Cierra was a story."

"Oh." Gary bowed his head sheepishly. "But why would Auntie P lie to us?"

"Why did you decide to take your lunch break now?"

Gary looked at his phone. "Auntie P sent me a text and asked me if I wanted to join her on the porch for lemonade."

"How many minutes passed between her text and your arrival?"

He shrugged. "Just a few."

I motioned toward the table. "And there were three glasses of lemonade waiting on us."

He cocked his head to the side. "I know I'm just a dumb handyman, but I'm not following you."

"Last week, Aunty P told me that you were single. Today, when she sees me walking toward the house, she sends you a text asking you to come to the porch. Five minutes after you arrive, she finds a reason to leave. Seem suspicious to you?"

"You think she's trying to set us up?"

I nodded. "Oh, I *know* she's trying to set us up."

Gary shifted uncomfortably. "Well… uhm… that's…"

Then it dawned on me, Gary had ended the conversation so abruptly on Friday because he realized I was attracted to him. Obviously, he didn't feel the same way. Though it wounded my pride, it gave me no excuse to be rude. So, I decided to smooth things over. "Why do people of that generation always assume people of our generation want to be fixed up?" I shrugged. "Maybe people in our generation are more independent, happier being alone."

Gary made a sound like air leaving a tire, "Pshh, yeah. I'm completely happy being alone." He balled up the brown paper bag that still contained his sandwich. "I gotta get back to work." He pushed himself to his feet and marched to the backyard.

As I watched him walk away, which by the way was a pleasant view, I muttered to myself, "What the actual hell?" He thought I was attracted to him, and he ran away. I make it very clear that I'm not attracted to him, he runs away. *This* is why I had given up on dating. Men were more trouble than they were worth!

When Zeus and Carly trotted around the side of the house, they rushed to me for attention. "At least somebody thinks I'm worth spending time with," I muttered.

The following day, at one o'clock sharp, I got a text from Aunty P. "Carly is driving me crazy. Can you bring Zeus down to run off some of her energy?"

After a morning of Zoom meetings, I was anxious to see a human being in person. I harnessed up my pup and headed to the Allen's house. As I approached, I saw Gary sitting on the top porch step, looking like a man being held hostage. I almost felt sorry for the guy.

"Imagine seeing you here?" I smirked.

Gary sat up straight. "Aunty P asked me to come to lunch on the porch."

I nodded in understanding. One did not say no to Aunty P.

She wagged her finger in Gary's direction. "We all need a little company, especially in these crazy times. I was watching the news; it may be October before we get back to normal."

I let Zeus off his lead and strolled up the walkway. "I thought you didn't want to spend time around people because of Cierra's rendezvous with her friends."

Aunty P shifted in her chair. "Turns out I heard things wrong yesterday morning. Her friends were all gettin' together, and Cierra was fit to be tied that her parents wouldn't let her go. She got grounded because of her sass and backtalk." She tugged at her earlobe. "You know how old ladies are, bad hearing, getting their stories all wrong." She looked at me over her glasses. "You two didn't stay out here and chat for very long yesterday."

I tried to sound casual. "You can't just throw two strangers together and expect there to be scintillating conversation."

"That's cause you two ain't old like me. You don't have the stories I have. Did I ever tell you about the time Malcolm and I took a riverboat cruise in New Orleans? Now they have real jazz down there, none of this cussin' and rappin' stuff." She talked for a good hour, telling stories about growing up in the Baltimore suburbs and vacationing in Africa.

Gary and I were totally captivated by her tales. When it was time for him to go back to work, I stayed on the front porch and talked with Auntie P.

She steepled her fingers. "So, why didn't you and Gary stay and chat a while yesterday? And I want the real reason; none of this 'we're strangers' stuff."

I let out a sigh. "When I mentioned that I thought you had left us alone for a reason, he got uncomfortable. I don't think he is interested."

"Why wouldn't he be interested? You are a young, beautiful, successful, confidant woman. Any man would be lucky to have you!"

"Maybe I'm not his type?" I nodded to my ebony skin. "Some people are not comfortable with interracial dating."

"Gary's completely fine with it. His ex-wife was black."

I know it's completely illogical, but hearing that Gary had an ex-wife made my stomach turn over. I searched my brain to come up with a talking point to change the subject. However, I didn't get a chance to speak. Two fur-covered shapes zoomed around the corner and began wrestling in the flowerbeds.

"Not my azaleas!" Aunty P squealed.

I yelled, "Zeus! Carly! Get over here right now!" Carly stayed put, but Zeus slunk over to me with his tail between his legs. He rolled over onto his back in a submissive pose. "Don't look all sorry now; look at all of the damage you two did!" I picked a piece of mulch from his fur. "I'll come back tomorrow to fix things, Aunty P, I promise."

~ ~ ~

The next day, I got a text asking me to come to lunch at the Allen's home. When Zeus and I arrived, Aunty P was not on the front porch, but Gary was. His white t-shirt was soaked with sweat, making it stick to his skin. It clung to his muscular shoulders when he moved. I shifted my eyes to his face before I started salivating over his physique, but that was no better. The way his shy blue eyes stared at me through his lashes was just as intoxicating. I swore under my breath. Why did he have to be so damn good-looking and so uninterested in me?

Gary fidgeted with his sandwich. "Hi, Jada."

I didn't trust my weak knees to carry me up the stairs, so I sat on the bottom step. "How's the patio coming along?" I asked.

"It's coming along nicely." He looked at the door. "Aunty P says she's making more lemonade and will be out in a few minutes." He motioned toward the three frosty glasses on the table. "I told her we didn't need any more, but she wouldn't listen."

"That woman doesn't give up." I chuckled to myself. "She reminds me a lot of my nana. Sweet as shoo fly pie but stubborn as a mule."

"Shoo fly pie?"

"You've never had shoo fly pie?" I rubbed my stomach. "It's got molasses, eggs, and brown sugar. My nana used to make the best shoo fly pie in the south. She taught me how to make it, but mine was never as good as hers."

He cocked his head to the side. "You're really close with your family?"

I nodded. "I lost my daddy when I was in my twenties in a car accident. Nana went not long after. It was too much for her to handle, putting her son in the ground. I have two sisters and my mom left, though. My mom's my best friend. I hate this stupid Covid stuff because I can't see her."

He squinted into the sun. "It's been hard on a lot of families."

Something about how the corners of his mouth sagged when he said families made my heart break just a bit. I wanted to ask him more, but I decided it would be better to change the subject. "Did you have any grand plans this summer that got ruined? Vacations? Tickets to watch the Nationals?"

He shrugged. "I had tickets to see *Hamilton* at the Kennedy Center."

"You had *Hamilton* tickets? Me too!" I screamed. "I was so bummed. My mom and I have been waiting years to see it, and when we finally get tickets, it gets cancelled."

Gary chuckled at my reaction. "You know you can watch it on Disney Plus?"

"Oh, I have, like a billion times. I have the entire score memorized."

Gary grinned. "What's your favorite song?"

"I love *Wait For It*."

Gary took a sip of lemonade and smiled. Then, he opened his mouth, and a haunting baritone voice sang, "Love doesn't discriminate between the sinners and the saints."

It took me a few moments to find my voice. "That was beautiful. You should try out for one of the local theater productions."

His cheeks turned as pink as his sunburned neck. "I'm no actor." He took another sip of lemonade. When his lips touched the frosted glass, it was the first time I'd ever found myself jealous of an inanimate object. "Get hold of yourself, girl." I silently chastised myself.

Gary sat the glass down with a thud. "I heard a rumor that when Hamilton premiered Lin-Manuel Miranda used dress in disguise and sneak into the audience to see how people were enjoying the show."

"I'd never heard that, but it sounds like something he would do." I stretched my legs out in front of me. "What's your favorite song from the score?"

"I really like the opener, but my absolute favorite is probably *You'll Be Back*. I love the King of England."

I was going to reply with something witty when Zeus trotted up to me and put his rough paws on my lap. "Hey there, pretty boy." I rubbed his ears. "Where's your girlfriend, Carly?"

"Carly!" Gary jumped to his feet. "I bet she's digging holes where I have the soil leveled out." He raced down the stairs. Right before he turned the corner, he looked over his shoulder. "Sorry to run off, but I gotta check on Carly. Thanks for having lunch with me."

Before I could reply with a pleasantry of my own, he was out of sight. I harnessed Zeus and started toward home. I was almost to my driveway when I realized that Aunty P never did come out for lunch. "That sneaky ol' lady," I mused as I booted up my computer for another Zoom meeting.

On Thursday, I didn't get an invite to lunch, but I headed to the Allen's at eleven anyway. Neither Aunty P nor Gary was sitting on the front porch when I arrived. I climbed the stairs and knocked on the front door. "Aunty P, do you want to have lunch?"

Her voice called from the kitchen. "I do. I do. Gary's working outback. Why don't you tell him lunch will be ready in a few minutes?"

I shook my head. That woman was relentless. I made my way around back, but the moment I rounded the corner, I stopped in my tracks. The backyard was unrecognizable. A gravel-filled, eighteen-inch depression had replaced an expanse of grass and flowerbeds. Gary was using a rake to level the stone.

"You're making a lot of progress," I yelled over the Poison song that was on the radio.

He jumped. "Jeez, Jada. You scared me."

"Sorry about that." I walked closer. "You've accomplished so much in just a few days. I'm impressed."

Gary took off his baseball cap and wiped the sweat from his brow. His shirt hung to his chest, and once again I admired the beauty of a workingman's body. I diverted my eyes before he caught me staring. "Aunty P wanted me to tell you she's making lunch."

The corners of his mouth turned up. "She is something else. I hope that when I'm her age, I have half of her spunk."

I laughed. "Spunk is an understatement."

"Speaking of spunk, I want to show you something." He pulled his phone from his back pocket. "I met this little lady last night hanging around a construction site, and I had to take her home with me."

I wouldn't have been more surprised if he had stripped to his undies and danced the mamba. And, if he HAD stripped to his undies, at least it would be a pleasant surprise. This was… this was… this was nauseating. Not only was I crushed that he'd hooked up with another woman, and I also never saw him as a man to brag about such things. I gave him a deliberate once over. "You want to show me a picture of your sexual conquests?"

Gary let out a thunderous laugh and held out his phone "Just look at the picture."

If he wanted to play this game, I'd play. "Give it here," I snarled as I grabbed the iPhone from his hand. My eyes widened as I looked at the raven-haired, green-eyed beauty staring back at me. The words spilled out of my mouth. "She is gorgeous."

"Ain't she though?"

I handed the phone back to Gary. "Did you know kittens are my kryptonite?"

A proud smile spread across his face. "I told you I missed having a furry companion. Well, last night I stopped by to see a buddy on the job, and this little thing crawled out from under a beam and strutted straight at me. Then she let out the most pathetic little meow you've ever heard. What could I do?"

The way he cradled the phone, as if it were the kitten itself, the cute dimple in his left cheek, the softness in his eyes, made my heart do that flip-flop thing you see in cartoons. I had to look away before I actually swooned "I never pegged you as a cat person."

He chuckled. "I'm not, or at least I wasn't until last night. This little fur ball has me wrapped around her tiny little paw. I need to stop on the way home and pick up scratching posts, some toys, and a litter box. For now, she's just using a shoe box lined with a garbage bag."

I made a face. "You are definitely going to need something better than that." Then, an idea hit me. "I have one of those litter boxes with a lid on it sitting in my basement. It's yours if you would like to have it."

Gary cocked his head to the side. "What will your cat use?"

"I don't have a kitty anymore. I had Bubba for sixteen years, but he passed away in 2017. That's when I adopted Zeus."

Gary looked to the oak tree where Zeus and Carly were laid out flat like pup-cakes. "It looks like you two get along pretty good."

I chuckled. "He's a sweet mutt." I looked at my watch. "I've got to get working on Aunty P's flower bed then get back to work. Why don't you stop by when you are finished here? I'm number 4321 at the end of the street."

"You sure you don't mind? I'll pay you for it if you like."

I saw this as a chance to reassure him that I understood where we stood. "Don't worry about it. It's what friends do."

There was the slightest twitch in his jaw, but he nodded and said, "I should be finished around six, if that works for you."

"Six works," I said then returned to the front flowerbed to repair the damage my mutt had done.

~ ~ ~

At 6:15, my doorbell rang. I opened my door to see Gary, masked and respectful, standing on my doorstep. I motioned for him to come into the foyer and turned to grab the bag of cat supplies. "I cleaned the litter box. However, some cats won't ever use a box that has been used by another cat, so I'd keep out that little shoebox for a while to see if she'll use this one." When I handed Gary the bag, I saw that he was pale, and his blue eyes were dull. "Hey, you okay?"

He made a dismissive gesture. "I'm fine. I got a little overheated."

"Why don't you come in, and I'll get you some water?"

"I'm fine." He swayed a bit.

Why were men so freaking stubborn? Well, nobody outstubborns Jada! I put my hands on my hips. "I said, walk your heat exhausted ass into my air-conditioned home and sit in that recliner while I get you some water."

Gary huffed like a teenager with attitude, but he obeyed. I brought him a glass of water, and he drank it in under a minute.

"Slow down. You don't want to make yourself sick." I tapered off my sass and refilled his glass. "Why didn't you just ask the Allens to come in and cool down for a bit? I'm sure they'd have let you."

"I didn't want to bother them." He shrugged. "To be honest, I don't feel comfortable going into people's homes with this Covid stuff, especially somebody as fragile as Aunty P."

"I think fragile is the last word I'd use to describe Aunty P." I sat on the sofa at the other end of the living room. "But I understand what you are saying. That's very respectful."

He looked at his hands. "That's the reason I didn't want to come into your home. I don't want to be the reason anybody gets sick."

I sat up straight. "You're not showing symptoms, are you?"

He pressed his lips into a fine line. "If I were showing symptoms, I would self-quarantine like any rational person."

I sat back on the sofa. "Sorry. I didn't mean to jump to conclusions. I guess I'm overly cautious."

He took a long drink of water. "We're all a bit on edge."

Zeus lumbered into the living room and realized we had a guest. He plopped his head in Gary's lap and waited for an ear rub.

I buried my face in my hands. "I'm sorry. He's such an attention hound."

"It's not a problem at all, but it does remind me that I have a special little lady waiting for me at home." He pushed himself to his feet. "Thanks, Jada. I needed somebody to strong-arm me into not acting like a moron."

"Anytime you need to be strong-armed, I'm your gal." I flexed my biceps. "Are you sure you're alright to drive?"

"I'm feeling a lot better, thanks."

I handed Gary the cat supplies, and we walked him to the door. Zeus whimpered as he drove away. "I know, boy." I sighed. "I feel the same way."

~ ~ ~

At eleven the next day, I headed toward the Allen's house. Aunty P wasn't on the front porch yet, so I made my way to the backyard. Gary was placing pavers. I let Zeus off his lead and did my best to keep my eyes off Gary's V-shaped torso.

His phone rang, and he looked up. "Hey there, Jada. I set an alarm so that I didn't miss lunch with the ladies."

"Lunch with the ladies, huh? Sounds like you are attending high tea." I laughed. "How's your sassy little lady? Have you thought of a name yet?"

He held out his phone. "Look at what she got into last night."

I flipped through pictures of the kitten on her back playing with string, of her mouth and whiskers covered in soft food, of her asleep on his oh-so-muscular bare chest. I handed the phone back before my eyes could pop out of my head. "Looks like she's adjusting well."

An adorable grin spread across his face. "She's something else, that's for sure. I think I'm going to name her Midnight, Middy for short."

"You're smitten with that kitten. So how does it feel to have your life ruled by a tiny female?"

"Much better than the last time." Gary put his phone in his back pocket. "You've never met my ex-wife."

"You were married?" Although Aunty P had told me, I pretended it was new information.

Gary shrugged. "Not the best period of my life, but yeah. I was married."

"What happened?" I put up my hands. "Never mind, that's a very personal question."

Gary looked at me sideways. "Do you want the story that I tell most people, or do you want the real story?"

"You choose."

He took off his baseball cap and wiped his brow. "The story I usually tell is that we were both too young to know what we were getting into and should have never gotten married. After ten years of trying, we decided to part ways."

"Sounds pretty normal."

A horse laugh escaped his throat. "The real story is that she couldn't see herself staying married to a man with no ambition or drive."

I cocked my head to the side. "No ambition? You own your own company."

"I own a landscaping company. I never went to college. I don't wear a suit to work. I have a farmer's tan and a sunburned neck. I come home with cement on my pants and dirt under my fingernails." He looked at his hands. "That wasn't her definition of a respectable husband."

I crinkled my nose. "She sounds like a peach."

"Peach? That's one word for her." He laughed ironically. "I tried everything I could to make her happy. We were building a house on the Potomac. It really stretched our budget, so I took on extra jobs. One day I came home early to surprise her, and I found her in the kitchen with our realtor." His Adam's apple bobbed up and down as he swallowed. "Let's just say, they weren't looking at countertop designs."

"I'm sorry she did that to you."

He clenched his jaw. "That wasn't the worst part; the divorce proceedings were worse."

"How could anything be worse than that?" I wondered out loud.

His eyes cloud over. "At our divorce hearings, she took every opportunity to point out that I was the only one in the room without a college degree. By the end of the process, I felt like I was nothing." A growl escaped his throat. "The way she and her lawyers glared at me. Do you know how it feels to have somebody look at you like you are less than human?"

It hurt my heart to see him like this. I wanted to reach out to him, but I didn't. All I could do was reply, "Yeah, I do."

He didn't look up. "I doubt that."

I lifted an eyebrow. "What is that supposed to mean?"

"Nothing." He turned his back to me. "Forget I said it."

There was a dismissiveness in his tone that rubbed me like sandpaper. Irritation replaced the compassion I felt.. "What if I don't want to forget it?" I mimicked his gruff tone.

He kept his back to me. "Can you just drop it, please?"

"No. I want to know what you meant."

When he wheeled around, he wouldn't look at me. "I'm just saying somebody like you would never understand."

"Someone like me?" I lifted my chin. "Are you telling a black woman working in corporate America that she doesn't know what it feels like to be treated as an inferior?"

Gary rolled his eyes. "That's not what I meant."

I put my hands on my hips. "Then explain to me exactly what you did mean."

His eyes widened with surprise, then narrowed. "I don't want to have this conversation."

"No, no, no. You don't get to make comments like that and then just disengage."

He crossed his arms over his chest. "Fine." He motioned toward my shoes. "How much did those cost?"

"Excuse me?"

"That shirt, was it more or less than $100?"

I didn't know if I was more angry or hurt. I'd accepted that Gary didn't have romantic feelings for me, but for him to use phrases like "people like you" then refuse to take ownership of it was too much. I thought he was different. I thought we were, at a minimum, friends. I blinked back the tears forming in my eyes. "How much this shirt cost is none of your damn business. However, I will tell you that I paid for it in cash, with money that I earned, in a job that I had to fight for!" My voice and my hands were shaking.

Gary jabbed a finger in my direction. "A job that you got because your parents sent you to college."

I took a step forward. "I went to college because my parents worked their asses off to provide a better future for my sisters and me."

"Exactly!"

I took another step. "You think I had it easy? How many times have you been mistaken for the secretary instead of the head of the department? How many times have you been told that you only got your position because of affirmative action or have somebody ask if they can touch your hair?" I took another step, to the point where I could reach out and smack him if I wanted to, and boy did I want to. "Please tell me, how many times have you been assertive in a meeting only to be asked if you should try this conversation at a better time of the month!"

He took a step back. "I never said you had it easy!"

I narrowed my eyes. "What would you know about not having it easy?"

He inhaled and exhaled slowly. When he spoke again, he was making a great effort to control his voice. "You have no idea what my life has been like."

"You're right I don't, because I don't make assumptions about people because of how they dress or where they live."

"Where they live?" He motioned around the backyard. "I grew up in a trailer park in Hank County, MD. Half the time we didn't have heat or running water."

I wanted to give a smart retort, but I held my tongue.

Gary continued, "Your parents worked hard to send you to college." He pointed to his own chest. "I have no idea who my dad is. My mom died when I was seventeen, and let's just say, she wasn't mother-of-the-year material when she was alive. I never had a chance to go to college, party with frat brothers, or earn a degree. Instead, my uncle took me to a construction site the day after my high school graduation." When he spoke again, it was with a concentrated effort. "I'm not saying your life has been easy, but don't' you assume for a single moment that you know anything about mine."

He turned back toward the patio. "I've got to get back to work." The gesture wasn't aggressive, but it was dismissive.

Though I wanted to argue more, tell him what a thick-headed ass he was being, I wouldn't give him the satisfaction of sticking around. I turned on my heel and marched toward the front yard. When I rounded the corner, I saw Zeus was sitting beside Aunty P on the glider rocker. "Woo, wee, sounds like you two were having some words," she hooted.

"He's a... He just..." I was too angry for words.

She scratched Zeus between the ears. "Gary's a good man."

"Do you know what he said to me?"

"Sweetie, the way you two were yelling, the entire cul-de-sac knows what he said to you, and what you said to him."

I didn't feel like rehashing the conversation. "I have to get back to work, Aunty P."

"Before you go, would you mind grabbing my sweater from inside, there's a nip to the air today?"

"A nip to the air? It's almost eighty-five."

"When you get old, like me, and your circulation isn't so good, you'll get cold too. Just you wait and see."

I grabbed Aunty P's cardigan from the hall closet. Then I collected my mutt and made my way home.

~ ~ ~

The next day, when the clock struck eleven, Zeus laid his paw on my lap. "Sorry, buddy. We aren't going for a w-word until later."

Zeus let out a pitiful whine.

"I know you miss Carly, but it's going to have to wait until after dinner."

He cocked his head to the side.

"Stop giving me that look. This has nothing to do with Gary. I have to call Mom." I picked up my phone. "See, I'm dialing right now."

Mom picked up on the first ring. "Jada Michelle, so nice to finally hear from you." She gave her usual greeting.

"Hey, Mom. How's the weather?"

"Hot as the dickens and no chance of letting up. How's my grand-pup?"

"He's being a pest. He wants to go on a walk, but I just don't have the time."

There was a clicking sound on the other end of the phone, then Mom said, "Sweetie, that was your Aunt Ruby. Do you mind if I call you this evening?"

I forced myself to sound polite. "Sure, Mom. I'll call tonight."

Before I had time to hang up, Zeus was already back at my feet. This time he had his harness in his mouth, something he'd never done before.

"You aren't going to leave me alone, are you?"

He yipped in reply and raced to the front door. The moment I had Zeus' leash hooked to his harness, he pulled me toward Aunt P's house. "Why is everybody doing everything they can today to get on my nerves?" I grumbled.

When we got to the brick colonial, I could see Aunty P sitting on the front porch. Luckily Gary was nowhere to be found I let Zeus off the leash and sat on the bottom step. "How're you doing today, Aunty P?"

She tightened her sweater around her shoulders. "I'm not feeling the best. Tired and worn out."

Before I could reply, Gary appeared on the front walkway. My stomach felt as if I'd swallowed molten lava. I gritted my teeth and asked Aunty P, "Is there anything I can get for you?"

"Would you mind handing me my lemonade?" she asked.

Happy to have a reason to turn my back on Gary, I climbed the porch stairs and reached for the lemonade. When I handed the glass to Aunty P, the lava in my stomach turned to ice. Her eyelids were heavy, her breathing was labored, and her lips had a strange grayish hint to them. I kneeled on the floor beside her. "Aunty P, is something the matter?"

"Just the usual aches and pains of an old lady." She made a dismissive gesture.

Gary rushed to my side. He knelt beside me and took Aunty P's hand. "Have you been having any shortness of breath? How about chest pains, have you had any pressure on your chest?"

"All old people get out of breath when they are walking a distance. We get indigestion, too!" She put her hands on the arm rests of the chair. "You two are making too much of this. I just need to rest for a while." She pushed herself into a standing position, and her knees buckled.

I caught her as she fell; she was as light as a child. I gently placed her back in the chair then looked at Gary. "Call Titus right now."

He did as he was told. Then I took my phone out of my pocket.

"Who are you calling?" he asked.

I mouthed the numbers, "9-1-1."

~ ~ ~

Kimberly arrived minutes after the ambulance. She left the car running and sprinted to the porch. "Aunty P," she cried. "I'm here. I'm right here."

A blond EMT put his hand on Kimberly's shoulder. "Ma'am, you need to take a step back and let us do our work."

Kimberly wiped at her cheeks and backed away. Chanta and Cierra ran to their mom. She wrapped her arms around the girls and tried to reassure them. "Aunty P's going to be alright. She's tough."

Titus arrived as the EMTs were placing Aunty P on the stretcher. He ran to his wife and daughters. "Gary gave me the details on the phone. Do we know anything else?"

Kimberly dabbed at her eyes and shook her head. Chanta fell into her father's arms. "I noticed she was acting strange this morning, but she said she was fine. I should have called you," she sobbed. "This is all my fault."

Kimberly rubbed her back. "This is nobody's fault, sweetheart."

Titus motioned to get the attention of the blond EMT. "Can you tell us anything? Is she going to be okay?"

He gave Titus a sympathetic smile. "Her Oxygen is low, and her heart rate is irregular. We're going to take her to Amanta General."

Titus looked at his family. "I'll ride with her and give you a call as soon as we get to the hospital."

"Sir," the EMT said. "I'm sorry, sir, but nobody can ride in the ambulance with the patient due to Covid restrictions."

Titus glared at the man as if he wanted to melt him on the spot. Kimberly put her hand on her husband's arm. "It's not his fault, dear."

Titus pressed his lips into a thin line. "OK, fine. I'll follow in the car."

The EMT held his palms out. "You won't be allowed in the hospital either, sir. Covid restrictions are…" he trailed off.

Cierra clung to her father. "So, she has to go alone, nobody can be with her? What if she gets scared or confused?" She buried her face in Titus' chest and sobbed.

The EMT put his hand on Cierra's elbow. "She's not alone. I'll hold her hand the entire way to the hospital, and once we get there, Amanta has the most amazing nurses in the country."

Kimberly wiped the tears from her cheeks and tried to give a brave smile. "Thank you."

Gary and I stood in the side yard as the ambulance pulled away. I wanted to hug the Allen family, tell them it would be okay, but I knew now was not the time. They needed to be alone as a family. Gary looked on the verge of tears, but after the way things had gone yesterday, I seriously doubted he would want comfort from me.

~ ~ ~

When the phone rang at seven a.m. the next morning, I jumped from my bed, stubbing my toe on the nightstand. I ignored the pain and grabbed the phone. "Unknown number!" I growled as I sank to the floor and rubbed my foot. Zeus ambled over and laid his head in my lap.

"I'm going crazy not knowing! Would it be intrusive for me to call?" I rubbed his ears. "Why am I asking for advice from a dog?"

My cell phone dinged. The same unknown number had sent me a text: *Hey, it's Gary.*

I called him back. He picked up before it had a chance to ring. "Hey, Jada. Sorry to wake you up so early on a Saturday."

"It's Saturday?" I rubbed my temples. "I completely forgot what day it was. Have you heard anything from the Allens?"

"Titus texted early this morning." He paused, and my stomach dropped. "The Cardio-Pulmonologist found a blood clot in her left lung. She's on blood thinners, but she's not out of the woods."

I covered my face with my hands. "This can't be real."

"Listen, I know I was a big asshole the other day, but would you mind if I came over? The Allens are a lot more than just an employer to me. I don't want to be alone."

He sounded so forlorn and lonely; I couldn't hold a grudge. "Sure, come on over."

"Would it be okay if I brought Middy? I feel bad leaving her alone, and Zeus is such a gentle dog."

"Zeus and I would love to meet Middy."

An hour later, Gary showed up on my doorstep. Under his arm was a fuchsia cat carrier, the litter box I had given him, and a bag of kitten chow. "I've got to get a few more things from the truck. Be back in a second."

I made breakfast while Gary introduced the animals. Within minutes, it was easy to see who was going to rule the roost. Zeus lay on the floor like a folded area rug while Middy nipped at his ears and played with his tail. By the time we finished breakfast, she had fallen asleep on his stomach.

I poured two cups of coffee. "Looks like they're going to be friends."

"Appears that way." Gary laughed.

"By the way, how did you get my number?"

"Aunty P gave it to me the day we had that argument in the backyard. I told her how bad I felt about losing my temper, and she gave me your number so I could apologize."

I gave a puckish smile. "I don't remember any apologies."

The tips of his ears turned pink. "I know. I'm sorry."

Why did he have to look so cute when he was being bashful? I pretended to be concerned with my coffee. "I wasn't exactly at my best either."

He looked to the corner where Zeus and Middy were sleeping in a heap. "If my cat and your dog can get along, I guess we can, too. Truce?"

"Truce." I took a sip of my coffee. "This needs a little something stronger than cream. You want any Bailey's or Frangelico?"

Gary's dropped his gaze. "No, thank you." He looked like a dog who had just been scolded.

I reached out and touched his hand. "You alright?"

He kept his eyes down. "The reason I'm so close to the Allen family... I'm not just the guy they hired to do their patio. That family has done for me than you will even know. Aunty P, Kimberly, Tutus, they were there when nobody else was."

I nodded. "They are good people."

"They're more than just that." He rubbed the back of his neck. "Titus is my sponsor. I'm an alcoholic. I've been sober for over three years. Aunty P is a large part of the reason I stayed sober."

It was my turn to feel ashamed. "Gary, I'm so sorry. I didn't mean to offer you liquor, at 9:15 in the morning!"

He lifted his gaze, but he wouldn't look at me. "You didn't know."

I squeezed his hand. "It was very brave of you to tell me."

"I'm not brave."

"I disagree. It takes a lot of courage to get sober and face those demons. My ex-boyfriend went through AA, you have to own up to a lot of stuff. That takes mountains of courage and strength."

His eyes became moist. "I needed to hear that."

I touched his cheek. "It's the truth."

His eyes met mine. Everything in the room faded, and all I could see was him. His piercing blue eyes, the brown stubble on his chin, his soft pink lips. My last shred of common sense flew out the window as I leaned in and kissed him.

When I tried to pull away, his muscular hands gripped my upper arms and pulled me to him. My body smashed against his rock-hard chest as his mouth covered mine. Before I knew it, we were in full make-out mode. I felt a fire envelop my body, then I felt a paw pressed into my side. I looked down to see Zeus standing on his back legs with one paw on me and one on Gary.

Gary smiled at Zeus. "Dude, help a brother out."

I suppressed a giggle. "I forgot to tell you; he doesn't like to be left out of hugs."

Gary scratched Zeus' ears. "Are you a jealous boy?"

"I don't think he's the only one." I looked in the living room. Middy was standing on the back of my couch, her tiny venomous eyes locked squarely on me. "I don't think she likes me," I said out of the corner of my mouth.

Gary let out a laugh. "She's fine." He walked over to the couch and reached out for the kitten, but she turned, stuck her nose in the air, and walked away. Then, she strutted to my favorite blanket and peed!

"That little brat!" I exclaimed as I ran to my blanket.

Gary walked to the couch, swooped her up in his hand, and held her so that they were nose-to-nose. "Midnight Rose O'Connor, that was not very nice! You apologize to Jada right now!"

I sidled up beside them. "That just goes to show how little you know about cats. They never apologize."

"I don't understand. She's used her litter box every single time, even when I'm not home."

"She's never had a female competing for your affection." I chewed my bottom lip. "Am I competing for your affection?"

Gary sat Middy back on the couch and looked at me. "I thought that kiss was a pretty good indicator that you had my affection."

"I thought you just wanted to be friends."

"Me? You are the one who used the f-word."

I threw my hands in the air. "When I hinted that Aunty P was trying to set us up, you acted like you were completely uninterested."

"I wasn't uninterested." He ran his fingers along my cheekbone. "I didn't think I'd have a chance with you."

I looked him up and down. "Have you looked in the mirror lately? Why on earth would I not be attracted to you?"

"You're a corporate CPA. You're brilliant, and educated, and cultured. I'm just a dumb hick—"

I put my forefinger on his lips. "Don't ever say that again."

Gary lowered his head. "But it's true."

I put my hand under his chin and lifted his head so that we were eye-to-eye. "You are NOT a dumb hick. You're a craftsman who builds things with his bare hands. You started with nothing and created your own business. Dumb hicks don't do that!"

He gave a one-shoulder shrug. "I know plenty of guys who started their own business."

"And how many of them had parents financing them?"

He ignored my question. "I only have a high school diploma, and I barely got that."

"Why are you so dang determined to put yourself down? I know plenty of people who hold a PhD who can't balance their checkbook much less run their own business. And intelligence? I remember every one of our conversations on Aunty P's porch – about epidemiology, theology, and this political circus that is threatening to swallow us whole." I kissed him gently. "You are a brilliant man who works with his hands, knows world affairs, and has a deep appreciation of the arts. I know how hard it was to get those *Hamilton* tickets."

He gave me a guilty smile. "What if I told you, I actually don't have that great an appreciation for the arts? I just wanted to see *Hamilton*."

I cocked my head to the side. "I'd say a lot of people want to see *Hamilton*?"

"It's more than that. The way Alexander Hamilton is introduced: a bastard, orphan, son of a whore." His voice grew deeper. "That's me. That's my story."

I took his hand and led him to the couch. "I can't imagine what it would be like to grow up with an absent dad and addict Mom."

He rested his elbows on his shoulders. "There are others who had it way worse."

"The fact that others have struggled doesn't diminish your experiences or pale your triumphs."

He hung his head. "It's not just how I grew up or my lack of pedigree. I'm afraid that when you see who I really am, you'll run for the hills. After Angie left, when I was drinking, the man that I was then—"

I held up my finger. "That's just it, the man that you WERE, not the man you are now."

"Yea, but—"

"No buts. We all have regrets, things for which we are ashamed. The beauty of all of this," I made a motion from myself to him, "is that we get to start anew with people who don't know our regrets and ugly parts. It's a clean slate, for both of us."

"But we aren't the same." He motioned to my living room. "I know how much these houses cost. I live in a one-bedroom apartment over my business. My truck is ten years old. My lawyer took everything in my savings account. I have nothing to offer."

"Do you honestly think I care about your apartment, or your truck, or if you can buy things?"

"Angie did."

"I'm not Angie." I put my hand on his forearm. "You offer me kindness, laughter, intriguing conversation. I don't care about things."

I gave him a tender kiss on the temple and felt a calm rush over me. Then I felt four tiny little nails pierce my calf. I looked down and saw a ball of black fluff climbing my leg as if it were a rope in gym class.

"Midnight!" I yelled as Middy clawed her way up my leg and finally settled into my lap. I rubbed her under the chin. "And I thought Zeus had jealousy issues!" I leaned back against the sofa cushions. "I guess if we are going to do this, I'll have to be satisfied with being the number two woman in your life."

Gary lifted the kitten and touched his nose to hers. "Little lady, we are going to have a conversation about boundaries."

We spent the rest of the day cuddled up on my couch. I introduced him to *Schitt's Creek,* and he introduced me to *Game of Thrones.* Around three, Gary's phone rang; though I could only hear one side of the conversation, I knew from the tears in Gary's eyes what was said. Aunty P had left us.

Though my heart was broken, Gary's was shattered. I had grown to love Aunty P over the past few months; she was a neighbor and a good friend. But to Gary, she was the mother he never got to have.

Over the course of the day, he told me stories about their relationship. When he was going to AA, Aunty P would call him every morning to make sure he was up and ready to go. She let him stay in her spare bedroom while he got his business back on track. On the nights when he didn't trust himself to not have a drink, she would stay up and tell him stories about marching in Montgomery..

When he was finally out of stories, he fell asleep on my sofa. Zeus, Midnight, and I curled up right beside him.

April 2021

With the roll out of the Covid 19 vaccine, the Allen family felt it was safe to have Aunty P's memorial. It was a brisk and beautiful day. When the wind blew, there was a nip in the air, but when the sun's rays shone down, it warmed you to the core. The tulips were in bloom at Tuscarora Park. I sat in a folding chair watching family members and friends take their turn at the podium sharing memories of the powerful woman.

Titus was the final person to speak. He folded his hands and began, "To say Aunty P was an amazing woman is a bit of an understatement. She touched so many lives in so many ways."

Murmurs of "yes, she did" came from the audience.

Titus continued, "When I tried to think of how to eulogize Aunty P, I felt a bit overwhelmed. How can you recap a life that was so full of adventure and love? So, I decided to focus on the four things I loved the most about Aunty P. First, she was smart. She graduated from Howard University with perfect marks and was one of the engineers who designed The Blueland tunnel. She knew everything from calculus to quilting, and she was happy to share her wisdom." He held up two fingers. "The second thing that comes to mind when thinking about Aunty P was her courage. During the Civil Rights movement, she and Malcolm canvassed the south registering people of color to vote. They faced the possibility of jail time, bodily harm, and even death so that voices could be heard. But she was unafraid because Aunty P was a woman of faith!" He smacked his palm on the podium for emphasis, and the crowd erupted with murmurs of agreement.

When the mourners were quiet, he continued, "Which brings me to point three. Aunty P followed Christ even when it took her to scary places. She didn't proselytize with her mouth. Instead, she showed Christ's love by showing compassion and tenderness toward others. I…" His voice broke. "I am one such person who is better off because of her kindness." He took a step back from the podium and wiped his cheeks.

When he resumed the eulogy, his posture had softened, and he was smiling. "The fourth thing about Aunty P is that she didn't mind meddling in the affairs of others."

A soft laughter broke out among the mourners.

"Aunty P considered herself a matchmaker, and she made some pretty fine matches." He smiled at his wife, Kimberly. "I know I'm forever grateful for her meddling." He looked out at the crowd. "Just out of curiosity, how many of you sitting in the audience found your soulmate because of Aunty P's matchmaking?"

I looked around; at least twenty hands were raised. I gave Gary a sideways glance, and in perfect unison we lifted our hands to the sky.

4

Quarantined with a Stranger

March 14, 2020

Dulles International Airport

"Move forward, please," a metallic voice boomed over the loudspeaker.

Dutifully, Elliot grabbed her paisley carry-on and moved six feet to the next blue square taped on the ground. She was almost free. Only two families stood between her and the next TSA agent. The first was an elderly couple wearing matching Union Jack t-shirts. The second family consisted of a couple in their forties and a teenage boy with greasy black hair barely hiding the acne erupting on his forehead.

The boy jerked his earbuds from his ears. "Mum, why do we have to stand in this bloody queue?"

His mom's wrinkled business suit and exhausted expression were telltale signs of the nine-hour flight from Heathrow they had all just endured. She pinched the bridge of her nose. "I don't know, Gareth, but complaining about it won't make it move any faster."

"Stupid pandemic," he muttered as he jammed his earbuds back in place.

The voice on the loudspeaker sounded again, "Move forward, please."

Everyone shuffled six feet to the next blue square and waited. Elliot checked her phone; nothing new. For a split second, she thought about texting her mom, Margo. But she knew that would lead to a deluge of questions and I-told-you-sos.

Margo had been against the European trip from the get-go. Elliot cringed remembering the conversation. "Why don't you ask the nice man in the townhouse next to yours to go with you?" Margo had insisted. "It's not right for a woman to go traipsing around Europe alone."

Though her mom's words were about the vacation, the judgment in Margo's voice communicated what she really meant: *It isn't right for a thirty-two-year-old woman to BE alone.*

Not for the first time, Elliot wished her relationship with her mother was different. She had desperately wanted to confide in Margo that Tristan, the nice man who lived next door, was the reason she was leaving the country. Six months ago, they had started a whirlwind love affair that made her dream of white picket fences and family vacations. She wanted to share the betrayal she felt when she came home from work three weeks ago to find him rifling through her jewelry box or the embarrassment she felt when she realized that Tristan was also a habitual gambler with some very nasty people after him. But Margo was more a fading socialite than a shoulder to cry on.

So, instead of confiding in family, Elliot cashed in all her vacation time and booked a first-class flight to Paris. Her first week in Europe was the stress-free escape she desperately needed, but as she was vagabonding around London, news broke that due to the spread of a nasty, respiratory virus that was making people very ill, all Americans were urged to return to the States.

The metallic voice pulled her from her thoughts. "Move forward, please." Elliot slid her cell phone into her back pocket and obeyed.

When it was finally Elliot's turn, she stepped toward the counter. An African American man in a blue TSA polo held up a finger. "One Moment, please." He wiped the counter with Clorox Wipes, then replaced his old gloves with a fresh pair. His tired brown eyes met hers. "Identification, please," he said.

Elliot reached into the front pocket of her purse and produced her driver's license and passport.

The man looked from her passport to her face and then back to the document. "Full name?" he asked.

"Elliot Madison McCoy."

He looked at his computer screen. "And Dulles International Airport is your final destination?"

"Well, after I leave the airport, I plan to go to my house in Harpers Ferry, West Virginia."

For the first time, Elliot noticed a woman in a pin-striped pants suit stood beside the TSA agent. Her black hair was pulled into a tight bun, accenting her round green eyes. She stepped in front of the agent. "Miss McCoy, I'm Candace Sandman, a representative of Heathrow Air. There's a situation that we must discuss."

Elliot rocked back on her heels as the glazed chicken she'd eaten on the flight churned in her stomach. "What's this about?" She tried to keep her voice calm.

Candace continued, "As you know, the virus known as COVID-19 is quickly spreading."

Elliot nodded. She'd spent most of the transatlantic flight on the CDC and WHO websites, enough to make herself rightfully freaked out. "I'm well-aware of COVID-19," she said. "It's all anybody on the plane could talk about."

Though her tone was from worry, she realized it could sound an awful lot like indignation, and unless you were a fan of body-cavity searches, one did not get indignant with TSA agents. She added in a sympathetic tone, "Everybody's on edge. I can't imagine how stressed out you must be."

A muscle in the woman's jaw flinched. "As I was saying, COVID-19 is an airborne pathogen that is passed from person to person. Those over the age of sixty and those with preexisting conditions are most vulnerable to the virus."

Elliot's stomach churned. "I don't understand why you are telling me this."

Candace's posture became even more rigid. "We regret to inform you that a member of the cabin crew from flight 456 is exhibiting symptoms of COVID-19. Because of his recent layover in Rome, he has been tested for the virus. We're asking all travelers arriving at our borders to consent to quarantine until the test results are back."

"Whoa, what—"

"We expect to have the test results in forty-eight hours. If you consent, you will be taken to a local hotel where your meals will be provided for you and all basic needs met. All of this will be paid for by Heathrow Airlines."

Elliot took a minute to process what she'd heard. "This can't be real. One of the flight attendants may have COVID?" she muttered to herself as she chewed nervously on her cuticle.

"Ma'am." Candace sighed impatiently. "The CDC recommends that you keep your hands away from your face and out of your mouth."

~ ~ ~

The cab ride to the hotel was painfully silent. Elliot was an extrovert by design, but when she was nervous, she suffered from a condition her mother had termed "diarrhea of the mouth." Words flowed from between her lips with no filter or purpose. However, after her first five attempts at engaging the driver in conversation fell flat, she finally gave up.

When they pulled up in front of a red brick building with a sign that read: "Home 2 Suites by Hilton," she tried one more time. "Do you know why they booked an extended-stay hotel?"

"Because they don't know how long you'll be here." The driver's voice was a deep baritone with a hint of an Eastern European accent.

"So, you do talk?" Elliot exhaled.

The driver shrugged. "Sometimes. I've been driving for sixteen hours straight, so I'm cranky."

"Oh, I'm sorry." Elliot gathered her purse. "I hope you get some sleep. Maybe I'll see you in forty-eight hours when you take me back to my car."

"Possible." The driver shrugged. "The man before you said that if flight attendant tests negative, you go home, but if the test is positive, you will be here for fourteen days, minimum."

"Nobody said anything about fourteen days?" Elliot choked out.

"This virus is nasty stuff." The driver looked at her impatiently. "Do you need any help with your bags?"

Elliot didn't' process what the man had said. Instead, she muttered to herself, "Fourteen days?"

As the cabby opened his door, she heard him mumble, "Fourteen days of sitting in a hotel, poor thing."

~ ~ ~

As Elliot walked into the hotel room, the smell of cleaning solution and fabric softener filled her nostrils. She parked her suitcase beside the painted white dresser and collapsed onto the closest queen-size bed. Sleep threatened to overtake her, but she knew if she napped now, getting rest tonight would be impossible. She grabbed the remote control from the nightstand and turned on the TV. The channel was set to CNN.

"Not the news!" She clicked through the channels and finally settled on HGTV. Just as *The Property Brothers* were showing the big renovation reveal, there was a knock at the door.

"Who is it?" she asked as she walked toward the door.

"My name is Curtis from concierge. May I speak to Mr. Elliot McCoy?"

She put on the mask she'd worn in the cab and opened the door. A man in his early twenties stood stiff as a board. His hazel eyes widened. "Oh, shit. You're not a man."

Elliot looked down at her pear-shaped body and then back to the man. "Well, aren't you observant?"

Curtis fidgeted uncomfortably with the cloth mask covering his nose and mouth. "Uh, we just assumed… Your name is Elliot…"

She crossed her arms over her ample chest. "Yes, my father gave me a boy's name, so what?"

His neck reddened. "There was an issue with the rooms. It seems we agreed to more people than we could house."

Irritation burned her veins. "So, you are moving me to a different hotel?"

Crimson climbed from the man's neck to his face. "Um, no. We actually can't do that. That could cross-contaminate. We need to keep all the passengers of flight 456 in one hotel." He dropped his gaze. "We're asking people if they would consider, for the greater good, having a roommate."

"You want me to share my room with a woman I've never met?"

"Not exactly."

Elliot crossed her arms over her chest. "Then what, exactly?"

The man kept his gaze on the ground. "With the name Elliot, we thought you were a male, so your roommate would be—"

"A man!" Her voice echoed off the walls, making both of them jump. She lowered her voice to a seething whisper. "You want me to share a hotel room with a strange man?!"

"Hilton apologizes for the inconvenience, but as you know this is an unprecedented—"

"Unprecedented," she snapped. "I'm so freaking sick of that word!"

To Elliot's surprise, Curtis threw back his head and laughed. It wasn't a laugh of amusement, but of exhaustion and defeat. "You know what, Miss McCoy," he threw his hands in the air, "you are right. 'unprecedented' is a horrible word. How about galactic shitstorm?" He rubbed his eyes with the heel of his hands. "Do you know I've been at work for over sixteen hours? My mom's on immunosuppressants. I can't even go home at the end of this shift." His voice rose half an octave, threatening to break. "Now the manager wants me to go room to room and ask people if they will agree to taking on a complete stranger as a roommate."

Pity filled Elliot's heart. "I can't imagine how much this must suck."

He turned to walk toward the elevator. "I'm sorry for wasting your time," he called over his shoulder.

"Curtis, wait," Elliot called after him. "Has everybody else accepted roommates?"

He turned in her direction but didn't lift his head. "Most have, but some haven't."

Elliot guessed she hadn't been the first to lose her temper with the young man. "If I say no, are there other men this guy can stay with?"

Curtis shook his head. "There are very few people traveling solo."

Traveling Solo. The words stung, but Elliot tried not to show it. She lifted her head. "What happens if I say no?"

"We'll move a cot to the ballrooms, and he'll stay there."

"So, if I say no, this guy is going to end up on roll away bed in a gigantic ballroom?"

Curtis nodded.

Elliot couldn't believe she was actually considering this. She chewed her bottom lip. "How do I know he isn't some kind of psycho?"

"The government ran background checks on all the passengers. We won't be pairing up anybody with a checkered past." He slapped his hand over his mouth. "Sorry, I wasn't supposed to mention that."

Usually, this would have seemed quite intrusive to Elliot, but with everything that had happened today, it seemed par for the course. She nodded, "Okay."

The young man's face lit up as if this were the first thing today that had gone right. "Are you sure?"

"Don't give me too much time to think about it, or I'll change my mind."

Curtis practically bounced up and down. "Thank you, ma'am!"

"How is this man going to feel about staying with a woman?"

"I'll give him the option of a cot in the ballroom and let him decide." Curtis gave me a half smile. "If it makes you feel any better, he seems like a decent guy. I spent several minutes chatting with him."

~ ~ ~

Twenty minutes later, there was a knock at Elliot's door. She glanced through the peephole, took a step back, rubbed her eyes, sure that lack of sleep and a plentiful supply of stress had made her hallucinate. She had expected a man to be standing in the hallway, but not this man.

Standing on the other side of her door was a six-foot-tall, dark brown-haired, green-eyed, broad-shouldered, narrow-waisted Englishman. Her roommate was Alfred Moffat: actor, philanthropist, and extremely attractive Brit.

She looked in the full-length mirror on the other side of the room and cursed herself for not putting on makeup or changing into something more alluring than a hoodie and faded yoga pants.

The gentleman knocked again. "Hello, is Elliot there?"

The deep baritone voice coupled with his British accent sent a shiver up her spine. She put her hand on the wall to steady herself. "This is Elliot," she responded. "Give me a minute, please."

She ran to the bathroom, applied a coat of mascara to her thin lashes, and spread gloss on her lips. Then she took a deep breath and opened the door.

Alfred was even lovelier than he appeared on screen. His high cheekbones, soft green eyes, and chestnut brown hair mixed in a heavenly symphony of handsome. A black t-shirt stretched across his broad shoulders, and though he was facing her, she could tell his blue jeans beautifully gripped his tight butt.

He smiled, revealing perfect white teeth. "I believe I'm your lodger for a few days." He extended his hand. "I'm Al."

She took his hand, which was soft and warm. "I'm Elliot."

"Thank you for allowing me to lodge with you."

Elliot looked away from his pale green eyes before her cheeks turned scarlet. "It's an unprecedented time. We're all doing things that we don't usually do."

"So, you don't usually have strange men knocking on your hotel room door?"

Her eyes shot back to his face. "Excuse me?"

Now it was his turn to blush. "Sorry, sorry. That didn't come out the way I intended it to." He ran his fingers through his hair.

"That flight always muddles my brain. I tend to say ludicrous things when I'm tired."

Elliot stood to the side, allowing him entrance to the room. "That's understandable; we boarded a plane over eleven hours ago. I think we are all pooped." She wanted to smack herself. Did she just say the word "pooped" to the sexiest man alive? And speaking of poop, was she going to be sharing a bathroom with this sexy star? How would she go knowing he was in the next room? Could she hold it for fourteen days if she had to?

Al's voice invaded her panicked thoughts. "So, you are from the States?"

"Yes." Elliot shook her head in an effort to get all thoughts of defecation out of her brain. "And you're from England?"

"How could you tell?" A playful smile made his dimples appear.

She looked him up and down. "Your outfit. Only men from England wear black t-shirts with faded denim."

Al wrinkled his brow and looked at his clothes.

"Just kidding." She gave a measured laugh. "It's the accent." Elliot's mother once told her that her authentic laugh, a high-pitched cackle, sounded like a Disney villain on cocaine. She definitely didn't want Alfred Moffatt thinking he was rooming with a hopped-up Maleficent.

"Sorry, I guess I'm too knackered to even get humor." Al gave a low chuckle and rubbed the back of his neck. "What part of the States---" He was interrupted by a knock at the door.

Elliot found Curtis, the bellhop, standing in the hallway with a room service cart beside him. Though Elliot wouldn't have thought it possible, he looked even more exhausted than before.

"Hello again," she said.

"How is everything, Miss McCoy?" he asked.

She looked from the young man to Al and back to the young man. "Things are fine and call me Elliot."

He nodded. "I have your meals. You ordered the chicken cordon bleu." He looked toward Al. "And, sir, you ordered a steak, medium rare?"

Both nodded. Curtis reached under the cart and pulled out a corked bottle. "As a way of saying sorry for the uncomfortable situation, the hotel sent up a bottle of wine to have with dinner. Do you like wine?"

"Yes," Al and Elliot said in unison.

As they ate, Elliot and Al made polite small talk. Then, exhausted and stomachs full, each climbed into their own bed and fell quickly asleep.

~ ~ ~

Elliot set the alarm on her watch to wake her up at seven a.m. Now that she was sharing a hotel room with one of *People Magazine's 100 Most Beautiful People,* the idea of showering, putting on makeup, and wearing a bra seemed a bit more pressing. So, she was quite distressed to roll over the next morning and see Al was already sitting up in his bed scrolling through his smartphone.

"Did I wake you?" he asked.

Elliot pulled her covers over her chest. "No, I was…" she muttered something about her internal clock.

"I tried to be as quiet as possible. But now that you're awake, do you mind if I turn on the telly? I'd like to see what is going on around the world."

His deep baritone voice and British accent were so sexy that it made red creep up her neck. She pulled the covers up to her chin. "I was just going to grab a quick shower, anyway. Do you know what time they're bringing breakfast?"

Al tapped a piece of paper on the nightstand between them. "They slipped this menu under the door last night. It says that they will deliver the food fifteen minutes after we order. If you tell me what you'd like, I can ring the kitchen."

Elliot ordered a ham and cheese omelet with orange juice and black coffee, then headed to the bathroom. After a scalding hot shower, she applied just enough makeup so she didn't look like a depressed basset hound and exited to the main room. The smell was heavenly: bacon mixed with French toast mixed with coffee. It was almost as heavenly as the man sitting at the table eating.

After the breakfast dishes had been taken away, Elliot decided to work on a pet project. She was tapping away on her laptop when she felt somebody standing behind her. She looked up to see Al peering over her shoulder.

"What language is that?" He pointed to her computer screen.

Elliot let out a giggle. "Trigonometry. I'm an architect. I'm designing a house for my sister as a wedding gift."

Al stuck out his tongue. "Sin, tan? Sounds like a religion lesson on a beach, and what is that funky symbol?"

"That's theta, it's a Greek letter."

"Ah, ha! I knew it was a foreign language." He sat at the foot of his bed. "I've got an idea. When you are finished working, I say we try to find something fun to do."

And this is when Elliot almost choked on her own tongue. Fun things to do? What did he mean? She could think of a few fun things to do with a sexy Brit, but she dare not say them aloud.

Forcing her breathing into a steady rhythm she said, "I'm all for fun, but I think our options for entertainment are limited."

Al raised an eyebrow. "I have a deck of cards from the plane."

"Cards!" A competitive smile replaced her embarrassed one. "I could definitely play a few games of cards."

They moved to the kitchen table where cut-throat games of Rummy, Crazy Eights, and Go Fish filled the afternoon. Through the playing, they talked. Elliot told stories about her family and pets. Al shared his experiences living in London. As they played game after game, Elliot began to see that the easygoing, friendly demeanor that Alfred Moffat presented during interviews was not an act. He was genuinely charismatic, friendly, and personable. And, despite the strange circumstances, Elliot found herself actually relaxing.

After they finished dinner, Al said, "We still have the bottle of wine. Would you like to open it, or should we ration, in case we are here for a while?"

"Actually," Elliot wrung her hands, "I have about seven bottles hidden in my luggage, plus some Patron, Grand Marnier, and a bottle of Grey Goose that I got in the duty-free store in Heathrow."

Al threw back his head and laughed. "Dear God, woman. That's a lot of alcohol."

Elliot held up her hands in a surrender pose. "I swear, I'm not an alcoholic. I was planning on drinking the wine when I was still touring the countryside. And the liquor from the duty-free store is SO much cheaper than any of the places in the US."

Al let out a laugh. "Oh, I meant no offense. In fact, I was thinking you are a wonderful quarantine partner. Too bad you didn't pick up any whisky at Heathrow."

"Oh no, that I got in Scotland. I believe it's a fifteen-year-old Glenlivet."

An appreciative growl echoed from his throat. "You have Scotch Whisky. I think I may be in love."

Elliot was glad she was facing the other direction, because if he had seen the color her face turned when he made that statement, she would have likely died of embarrassment. "You, um, like whiskey?" she finally managed to mutter.

"I do." Al laid down the cards in his hand. "I was being honest, though, about what I said."

Elliot's heartbeat drummed so fast that she could hear it thudding in her ears. He meant what he said? He thought he loved her? After only one day, he thought he loved her. Was this a ploy to get her into his bed? Not that she was opposed to the idea...

Al continued, "I mean, I'm glad you are my quarantine partner."

Of course, that's what he meant.

His moss green eyes twinkled. "When I was told I would be quarantined with a stranger, I was less than thrilled. But I have enjoyed myself today. I think that if we were under different circumstances, we'd probably be friends."

"I think you're right, about the friend thing." Elliot chewed her lip. "And as your friend, there's something I feel like I should tell you." She looked him squarely in the eye. "Because I think honesty among friends is very important, Mr. Moffat."

Al leaned back in his chair and rested his hands in his lap. "So, you do recognize me?"

"You're quite popular on this side of the pond." Elliot nodded. "Are you disappointed that I recognized you?"

"No," there was a tinge of sadness to his voice, "but I did like the idea of being just Al, a guy hanging out with a friend."

"Why can't you still be just Al, hanging out with a friend?"

Al gave a lop-sided grin. "That's a very good question."

~ ~ ~

The next morning, the hotel phone rang at 7:30. Alfred, who was already awake, answered.

Elliot listened to the one-sided conversation.

"Yes, this is he. No, I see. Drat. Thank you." He hung up the receiver and flopped back on his pillows.

"Is everything okay?" Elliot asked.

"That was the airline. The flight attendant tested positive. So, we're stuck in this hotel for another twelve days."

Elliot pulled her pillow over her face. She was annoyed about being kept within these walls, but she was giddy at the idea of spending another twelve days with Alfred Moffat.

After she had revealed she knew his true identity, they'd stayed up talking until after midnight. They talked about their experiences in school, their political and religious inclinations, and funny stories from their childhood. He told her humorous stories about his time on the set of *Purple Iris*, and she had asked him things she always wanted to know about being a movie star.

Alfred pushed himself into a seated position. "Well now that we know we're going to be here for a while, what do you suggest we do today?"

Elliot uncovered her face. "I guess I should email my work."

"Sounds like fun." Al smirked.

Elliot sighed. "As fun as a barrel of type-A monkeys." She grabbed her laptop from the nightstand and logged on. She felt a hot anger rise in her chest as she read the first message.

"Are you freaking kidding me?" she screeched.

Alfred sat up straight. "What is it?"

"A major project that I was supposed to spearhead when I got back from vacation has been postponed."

"I'm sorry."

She slammed her laptop closed and threw it onto the nightstand. "This was supposed to be my first big project, my chance to prove myself to the CEO. Now the office is shutting down for the next week so they can find a way to deal with this stupid virus!"

"That is truly disappointing news." Alfred pushed himself to his feet and started pacing. "You need a distraction."

Elliot motioned to the four walls. "Again, our options are limited."

Al grabbed his laptop from the kitchenette. "I've got an idea." He had an impish grin on his face. "Marvel, Tolkien, *Harry Potter*, or *Star Wars*."

Elliot cocked her head to the side. "Excuse me?"

"A movie marathon! What will it be? The six Tolkien, all eight *Harry Potter*, all twenty-three Marvel, or all ten *Star Wars*? It's lady's choice."

This child-like excitement in his eyes made her smile. "I'm not a huge *Star Wars* fan, so no to that one."

Alfred's face wrinkled like he had just smelled something rotten. "Not a *Star Wars* fan? Seriously? Over dinner, you said you were a science fiction geek."

Elliot pretended to pout. "I am a geek. I love the *X-Files*, *Dr. Who*, Tolkien, *Harry Potter*, Marvel, and *Star Trek*. I just can't get into *Star Wars*."

Alfred shook his head in mock disbelief. "I just don't understand Americans."

"And I'll never understand why the British drink warm beer."

Al threw his hands in the air. "It's not warm. It's cellar temperature."

"Which is still not cold as it is from a tap!" Elliot shot back.

Al pointed a finely manicured finger at her. "Fine, just for that jab, I get to decide on what we watch."

Elliot rolled her eyes. "And what is your choice?"

"Marvel." Alfred connected his computer up to the TV and cued the movie. "We'll start with *Iron Man*."

"What about breakfast?"

Al tapped his finger on his chin. "Right, breakfast first."

They watched *Iron Man* and *The Hulk,* then broke for lunch. By dinner, they had finished *Iron Man 2* and *Thor.*

"I have a question." Elliot tilted her head. "But I don't want to offend you."

"Well, that makes me nervous." He took a deep breath. "What is it?"

"You were in that romantic comedy with Chris Evans a few years ago?"

He scrunched his brow. "Yeah?"

"Is he as nice in real life? I mean, every time I see him interviewed, he seems so humble and pleasant."

Alfred crinkled his nose. "He's a complete dick."

Elliot sat bolt upright. "You're kidding."

"Yes, I'm kidding." A deep laugh exploded from his throat. "Chris is one of the most genuinely kind people I have ever met. Why did you think that would offend me?"

Elliot shrugged. "I don't know. You probably get sick of being asked about other actors, movies, or TV shows. I don't want to be one of those annoying fan-people."

"I don't mind talking about my work with you. I don't get the vibe that you'll run to TMZ with all the sordid details of our time together. What else do you want to know?"

She thought for a moment. "Who is a dick in real life?"

"Katherine Heigl is a real diva. Ed Norton was a bit rough. Bruce Willis had his moments." He chewed his lip. "What kind of reputation do I have? How do I come across in interviews?"

"You?" Elliot gave a shrug that she hoped looked nonchalant. "You come across as incredibly intelligent, well-spoken, socially conscious, and humble."

"Yes!" He snapped his fingers. "The act is working?"

Elliot giggled. "Yes, because our time together here has been dreadful. You're a complete ass, a high functioning sociopath."

Alfred started to reply, but then his phone rang. He crossed to the kitchen table to pick it up. "It's my publicist." He huffed as he clicked the "Talk" icon. "Hey, Ben, what's up?"

The look on his face immediately turned from annoyance to disbelief. "What!" he yelled into the phone. "Is this a sick joke?" He collapsed into a chair. "No, sorry, I know you would never… When did you find out?"

Elliot could hear the mumble of the conversation's other half as Albert ran his fingers aggressively through his hair. Something was obviously wrong, and she felt like a total voyeur just sitting her watching, but something kept her rooted in place.

Finally, Albert spoke again, "Keep me updated." He ended the call, pushed himself to his feet, then hurled his phone across the room. It hit the wall with a sickening crack.

Elliot watched the phone catapult across the room and flinched at the sound of smashing glass. When she looked back to Alfred, his rage was gone; replaced with pure anguish. He collapsed and covered his face with his hands.

Elliot rushed to him and placed her hand on his shoulder. "Alfred, what is it?" When he didn't answer, she asked, "Would you like me to leave you alone?"

"Please stay," he whispered.

He started to cry, gut-wrenching sobs that shook his entire body. Acting on instinct, Elliot knelt in front of him and put her hand on his knee. To her surprise, he reached for her. Holding her in against him as he wept on her shoulder. They stayed like that until his sobs became soft sniffles. When he finally pulled away, her sweatshirt was soaked.

He wiped his cheeks. "Thank you, that was extremely…" he trailed off.

"You looked like you could use a friend." Elliot pulled the other chair beside his and rubbed his back. "Do you want to talk about it?"

"I'm sure you'll hear all about it, anyway." He stared at the ceiling for a long moment then exhaled. "I used to be on a detective show, *The Magician*. My co-star was this bloke named Will."

"I remember, you and Will Remey would solve cold cases from the eighties."

Al nodded. "The actress that played Will's wife, Tina McMahon, tested positive for COVID-19 two days ago."

"I'm sorry. How is she doing?"

"She's dead."

Elliot stopped rubbing his back. "Dead? That doesn't make sense. She was young and healthy." Then Elliot remembered something that her stomach turned to lead. "Didn't she and Will have a baby recently?"

Alfred wiped his nose. "A baby girl named Rosie. She just turned two. I'm her godfather."

"I'm so, so sorry. I wish there was something I could do."

Alfred pointed to an empty glass. "Could you make me a stiff drink?"

Elliot mixed a little orange juice with vodka, then sat beside him again. She held his hand while he told funny stories about shooting on the set of *The Magician*, how he watched Will and Tina's romance blossom, and that he felt honored to be named Rosie's godfather. They talked until almost midnight.

When Alfred was exhausted, he looked at Elliot. "Thank you. You've been so kind. I feel like such a baby, but…"

"But what?"

"I don't want to sleep alone. If that makes you uncomfortable, I fully understand."

Elliot put her palm on his perfect cheek. "It doesn't make me uncomfortable."

Alfred curled up in a little ball, and Elliot lay behind him with her arm draped over his torso. She could feel his heartbeat under her palm, but it was what she was feeling in her own heart that terrified her.

~ ~ ~

The next morning, Alfred and Elliot slept right through breakfast. When they finally awoke around ten, Elliot ordered room service while he showered. After the dishes were cleared, he looked at his watch and sighed. "I guess it's time to make the call."

"The call?"

"Will." He rubbed the back of his neck. "I'm a bloody awful friend. I should have rung him last night."

Elliot reached across the table and took his hand, a gesture that seemed so natural. "It's like they tell you when you're flying, 'Secure your own oxygen mask before helping others.' You needed to process it yourself before you could be of any comfort to him."

Tears filled his eyes. "I don't know if I have fully processed it yet."

"Several years ago, I lost a coworker, a friend, very suddenly. He was only twenty-five. It took me way more than one day to wrap my head around the loss, the grief." She looked out the window. "Then three years ago, I lost my dad. He was eighty-six and had multiple organ failure." She shook her head. "What I mean to say is that, when it is sudden, when you aren't expecting it, grief is very different. Losing my dad was way worse than the loss of my friend, but because it wasn't out of the blue, it was somehow less painful. Or perhaps it was the same pain just drawn out over time." She chewed her lip. "I'm sorry; I'm rambling. My point is, there's no right or wrong way to behave when you lose somebody you love."

Alfred tightened his grip on her hand. "I know I've said this before, but I truly mean it." His moss green eyes pierced right through her. "I'm so glad you are the person I got quarantined with."

~ ~ ~

When Alfred made the call to his friend, Elliot excused herself to take a shower (and to poop- she was human after all). When she turned off the hot water, she could still hear his deep voice. She dressed, then looked in the mirror and mumbled, "As long as I'm in here, I might as well make myself look presentable for the first time." She tamed her frizzy locks, then applied foundation and mascara. When she finally heard silence from the main room, she exited.

Alfred was sitting on his bed with his head in his hands. She sat beside him and put her hand on his knee. "How's he doing?"

"He's rightfully distraught. Thankfully, his mum has come to help with Rosie while he sorts things out. The media is clamoring for interviews, and he must issue a formal statement today." He balled his hands into fists. "They cannot even leave the poor man alone to mourn his wife."

"That's hideous."

Alfred raised his head to look at her. His lips curved in a slight smile. "You look different. Is there a reason for this?" He made a motion toward her head.

Elliot's pulse pounded in her ears. Did he think she'd misinterpreted his request to accompany him to bed last night? Would he think the makeup was an attempt to appear more alluring? She cleared her throat. "No reason. I had over an hour in the bathroom, and I thought I'd try some of the makeup I purchased in Paris. I mean I've been quite a ragamuffin the past few days."

He cocked his head to the side. "It's nice, but I think I prefer the ragamuffin look." He shrugged. "Maybe because in show business, everybody is so made up all the time. Half the actors I work with have more plastic in them than a bottling plant, and everybody walks around with so much stuff on their face you can hardly see who they truly are. Natural is… refreshing."

She looked away. "Thank you."

He looked. "I wish we could go outside. I need a distraction."

"We could finish the Marvel movie marathon. I know it's not as good as getting outside, but it could distract you for a while."

"I like that idea."

They sat on Alfred's bed and shared bag after bag of microwave popcorn while the different Avengers saved the universe. After dinner, when the credits to *Guardians of the Galaxy* were rolling, the red wine won Elliot over, and she fell asleep.

When she awoke the next morning, Alfred was snoring quietly beside her. She propped herself on her elbow and studied his face. With his high cheekbones, rounded jaw line, and slightly receding hairline, he didn't look like the typical Hollywood heartthrob. Yet, he had a ravenous female following.

But when Elliot looked at him, she saw so much more than his hypnotic green eyes, smooth skin, and lean torso. She saw a man who was intelligent, kind, empathetic, and humble. A man who had every opportunity to be a cocky diva but chose to not use his celebrity privilege. She saw a man who was hurting over the loss of a friend, a man she wanted to wrap in her arms and protect from the pain.

She stared at the ceiling and reprimanded herself. *You can't do this. You're in this hotel room with him for another ten days. If you don't get these girlish notions under control, you're going to get your heart broken.*

She slid quietly from under the covers and went to her own bed. She was in the middle of checking her email when Alfred stirred.

"Hello, friend." He smiled.

The butterflies in Elliot's stomach started to flutter, and the nervousness came right back. She averted her eyes. "Do you want me to order breakfast?"

"Breakfast sounds lovely."

After a round of waffles, mimosas, omelets, and toast, Alfred's phone dinged. "Ah, ha!" he looked at his phone, "I've been waiting for this."

"What?"

"You Americans have this store called Target. Well, I found out yesterday that they'll deliver to our hotel room. I ordered a few things, and they are on their way!"

Twenty minutes later, a bell boy with a surgical mask and a trolley of boxes stood in the hallway. "Your order arrived, Mr. Moffat."

Elliot's jaw dropped. "What did you order?"

"A few things: snacks, an x-box, a Nintendo Switch, *Trivial Pursuit, Ticket to Ride, Cards Against Humanity*, and two gaming chairs."

"That's a lot of stuff!"

The bellboy turned to Alfred. "The other Switches are being delivered to each room."

"You ordered Nintendo Switches for every single room in the hotel?" Elliot gasped. "There are over one hundred rooms in this hotel!"

"One hundred and twenty guest rooms. And two different families have been situated in conference rooms."

"You bought one hundred and twenty-two gaming systems?"

"I bought one hundred and eighty. I figured the hotel staff had to be getting bored."

The busboy smiled behind his mask. "And we appreciate it, Mr. Moffat."

Alfred nodded in acknowledgment. "The staff gets to keep theirs, but I will sell the others on eBay at the end of the quarantine. Proceeds will be donated to a food bank."

"The local Target had one hundred and eighty switches on hand?"

Alfred shook his head. "Not exactly. When I told the manager what I wanted to do, she called other stores in the area and had them shipped to her store. It was a team effort."

"Eventually, I'm going to stop being surprised by you." Elliot collapsed onto the bed. "But today isn't that day."

The busboy turned on his heel, and the two got to work putting together the gaming system. By lunchtime, they were battling it out on *Mario Kart*. However, when they tried *Call of Duty*, Elliot found herself woefully underskilled.

After the dinner dishes were taken away, Alfred said, "Why don't we try a board game?"

"I refuse to play *Trivial Pursuit* with you."

He gave mock offense. "Why?"

"Because you're brilliant."

"I'm not that smart, and this is my fifth drink. I'm halfway to being pissed." He lifted his glass.

"Why are you pissed?"

"Because I've had five drinks." He all but added a teen-worthy *duh* to his statement.

"You don't seem like an angry drunk?"

Alfred let out a loud cackle. "Pissed means drunk, you silly Yank." He exaggerated his accent. "But I have a question for you."

Elliot put her palm to her chest. "I'm just a silly Yank, but I'll try to answer."

"What makes you think I'm smart?"

Elliot, who was on her third drink, didn't guard her words like she normally would. "I told you that I recognized you, but I never told you," she lowered her eyes, "I'm actually a pretty big fan. I make it a point to watch you when you are on talk shows like Graham Norton. I can tell by the way you answer things, you're extremely intelligent."

Alfred swirled the Patron in his glass. "Cleverness is appealing?"

"You know what they say, never underestimate the sex appeal of a man with a gigantic," she gave a mischievous grin, "vocabulary."

She saw a hint of pink in his cheeks. "I'll keep that in mind."

~ ~ ~

That night, as the credits to *Guardians of the Galaxy 2* were running, Alfred took Elliot's hand. "Today's been a horrid day, but you've kept my mind occupied. Thank you."

"You're welcome."

He looked at her, his eyes boring through her like a laser. "When you look at me, do you see Alfred Moffat, the actor, or do you see Al, the guy who yells at video games and sucks at *Go Fish?*" His voice was husky and his words slightly slurred.

Elliot's pulse quickened. "I see both. You're one and the same, two sides of the same coin."

He moved closer. The smell of tequila on his breath burned her nostrils. He ran his knuckles along her cheekbone. "Which side of the coin are you looking at now?" Before she could answer, his lips were on hers. It was a soft kiss, gentle and unsure. After a moment, he pulled away. "Was that too forward?"

"Not too forward." Elliot touched her lips, still wet from the tequila on his. "But you are drunk."

Alfred gave an exaggerated eye roll. "What does that have to do with anything? Drunks and children tell the truth."

"Not always."

"Well, it is now," he protested.

She stared at the vodka drink in her hand. If she looked at those hypnotic green eyes, it would be her undoing, and she'd lose all her resolve. "Sometimes, alcohol can create emotions that may not actually be there when we are less inhibited."

Alfred pushed himself onto his feet, wobbling a bit before righting himself. He flung his arm toward the door of the hotel room. "From the moment I walked through that door, we fit together like the spokes in a wheel. You held and comforted me when I cried. We play and laugh together. Why deny what is obviously in front of us?"

And just like that, the fantasy Elliot had been living for the past days evaporated, and cruel reality crashed in. She swallowed hard before she said the words they both knew to be true. "You are an internationally celebrated actor. You are one of *Glamour Magazine's Sexiest Men Alive*. Trust me, I have that edition in my bedroom."

"So?"

Elliot motioned up and down her body. "I'm a plain-Jane, size-twelve American who isn't special in any way."

"You're special in every way." The sincerity in his voice made her chest ache.

"I'm not. I'm as ordinary as they come. I have a list of men who would testify to that fact. Men who had three other girlfriends while swearing their love to me, men who had hidden addictions, and men who were still living in their mothers' basements." She swallowed back the lump forming in her throat. "They would each be happy to provide you with a list of why boring old me is not enough to hold their attention."

"Then those men were bloody morons. In fact, I'll say they weren't even men. They were boys, spoiled wee boys." He pushed a strand of hair behind her ear. "And you, my dear Elliot, deserve a man."

Those words coming from any man could make a woman melt but coming from his perfectly pink lips and in that oh-so sexy British accent… it was almost her undoing.

Almost. She knew all too well that promises and pretty words whispered in the middle of the night too often evaporated with the morning light. She forced herself to pull away.

Alfred frowned. "You don't believe me?"

The hurt in his voice wounded her, but she stood her ground. "Fine. I'll make you a deal." She lifted her chin. "If you still feel this way tomorrow, when you're sober, tell me then. Say these beautiful, amazing words to me again, and I'll believe you."

~ ~ ~

Though Elliot slept horribly, she was wide awake at six a.m. She looked at the bed beside hers. Alfred was muttering in his sleep and fidgeting restlessly. He had rolled and thrashed until the sheets were wrapped around him like a mummy. She fought the urge to go to his bed, wake him from the nightmare, and hold him in her arms. But she knew her limits. The past two mornings had felt too natural waking up next to him. The way her heart had pounded last night when he'd kissed her, she knew she was treading on dangerous ground.

Desperate for a distraction, she grabbed her laptop. The moment she opened Facebook, she saw a private message from her mother: *Why did I have to find out from your SISTER that you're back in the States?! She said you're quarantined in a hotel, is this true? God forbid you text your mother and let her know what's going on. Jordan told me not to say I told you so, so I won't. Message me when you get this.*

"Just what I didn't need to hear," Elliot grumbled. She closed the Facebook tab without replying and logged onto her work email. What she read there didn't make her feel much happier. Management was scrambling to find ways for employees to telecommute until the virus was under control, but no decisions had been made. She was to check in daily until a decision was reached. She typed an obligatory "checking in" email, then browsed Amazon for a few hours. After adding a new welcome mat, shower curtain, and the latest book by A. K. Huey to her virtual cart, she closed her laptop.

Alfred stirred at the sound. "What time is it?"

"A little after nine."

He rolled over and groaned. "My bloody head." He put a pillow over his eyes. "Why is it so damn bright in here?"

Elliot looked around the room and noticed that the only light was from the small lamp beside her. Instantly, she clicked it off. "You had quite a bit of tequila last night." She looked at the kitchen table where the empty bottle sat.

"I haven't been that pissed since college. I'm a bloody moron."

Elliot's heart sank. There had been a part of her, though incredibly small, that hoped he hadn't been as drunk as she thought, that he had meant the things that he said. But now he was admitting it; he had been sloshed. He probably wouldn't even remember what he said or the kiss. She inadvertently touched her lips, remembering the feel of his lips on hers.

He removed the pillow from his face. "I should know better than to drink like that."

Although Elliot wanted to despise him for playing with her emotions, she couldn't. She put her laptop to the side. "The past few days have been quite trying. You got quarantined in a foreign land and lost a friend to a vicious disease. It hasn't been an easy time."

"Still, I should know better than to…" A look of horror crossed his face. He untangled himself from the sheets, and with the speed of a jaguar, ran to the bathroom. Within seconds, the muffled sounds of retching could be heard throughout the hotel room. Elliot closed her eyes and suppressed her own gag reflex.

When Alfred walked back into the room, his face was covered in sweat. "Bloody, effing moron," he grumbled as he climbed under the covers.

Elliot suppressed a giggle. He was one of the most suave and richest men in the world, but hangovers were a great equalizer. "Would you like me to get you a coke or some crackers?"

He looked at her with hound dog eyes. "Would you?"

She put in a call to the kitchen for soda and saltines.

After he had kept those down, he asked, "Could you do me a favor? In my shaving kit, there are these little pouches of white powder."

Elliot shot to her feet. "Excuse me?"

"Not that white powder." He rolled his eyes. "They're electrolytes. Can you mix one of those powders in a glass of water for me, please? I'm dehydrated."

Elliot laughed. "Sure thing."

By lunchtime, Alfred was feeling slightly better, and the two resumed the Marvel movie marathon. They were still sitting at the dinette table watching the news on BBC America when Al pushed himself to his feet and stepped in front of the TV, blocking her view.

"You make a better door than window," Elliot said as she craned her neck to see around him.

"You are an insufferable woman, you know that?"

Elliot's sat up straight. "What on earth are you talking about?"

"I've been waiting all day for you to say something, but I can't do it anymore." He crossed his arms over his chest. "Are you really going to pretend like last night didn't happen?"

"I didn't think you remembered." Her voice was barely a whisper.

He sat at the table across from her. "I remember everything." He ran his fingers up and down her forearm. "You said: *If you still feel this way tomorrow, when you're sober, tell me then. Say these beautiful, amazing words to me again, and I will believe you."*

Elliot chewed her bottom lip. "You do remember."

"I'm hung over, but I'm definitely sober." His fingers intertwined with hers. "Do you believe me now?"

She lowered her head. "I don't know."

His mouth opened and closed like a trout taken from the stream. He pulled his hand away. "What have I done to make you distrust me so?"

Elliot focused on the outdated chandelier, anything to keep from looking into those moss-green eyes. "Do you know how many times you've made me cry? How many times you've—"

His spine went straight. "When on Earth did I make you cry?"

Elliot held up a finger. "The last act of *Hamlet*, when your dog died in *My Mutt and Me*, the season finale of *Iron Ivy*, when you guest-starred on *Dr. Who*..." she counted the instances off on her fingers. "You're an amazingly gifted actor."

"You think I'm acting?" He slammed his palm on the table. "Why? To get you into my bed?"

Elliot swallowed hard. "No."

The look on his face changed from anger to confusion. "Then what is it?"

Tears threatened to spill onto her cheeks. "It's not what you are; it's what I am." She shredded the edge of the paper napkin that came with their meals. "The man before you made me believe I was the most special woman in the world, then stole my grandmother's engagement ring to pay off gambling debts. The one before him convinced me I was the woman he wanted to build his life with, to be the mother of his children." She let out an ironic laugh. "Too bad he already had a wife and two beautiful little boys."

"Elliot—"

She held up her hand to stop him. "None of these men had Oscars or BAFTAs, but they were amazing actors; they made me believe." She stopped talking before the tears came.

He took her hand. "Two nights ago, when I was curled up in the fetal position, sobbing, was I acting?"

She shook her head. "No."

"You lay beside me, wrapped me in your arms, and comforted me. Was that an act on your part?"

She jerked her hand back in indignation. "No!"

"Believe me, I have met some of the best swindlers you could imagine. Some of them in the business, and some were not. You have no comprehension about how careful I must be about who I allow into my life."

Elliot let her head drop. "I never thought about that, how difficult it must be for you to find people you can trust."

"Harder than you realize." He put his finger under her chin. "And in my hubris, I assumed I was the only one who had that problem." The sincerity of his words was written across his face, and it melted her heart. "I'm not asking for promises or commitment. All I am asking for is that you allow me in, just a bit."

He leaned across the table, and she lifted her lips to his. Though the kiss began soft and gentle like the night before, it quickly evolved into a desperate hunger. Alfred walked to her side of the table, and she stood to greet him. A soft growl sounded in his throat as her body melted against his. She began unbuttoning his shirt, but he pulled away.

Her heart sank. "Did I do something wrong?"

He rested his forehead against hers. "No, everything you've done has been right, deliciously, tenderly, amazingly right." His breath tickled her neck. "But we're adults, and we need to approach this as adults. I want to make sure we're both on the same page as to where this is going."

Of course, this amazing, suave, gallant man was ensuring consent. It made him that much more irresistible. She kissed his neck. "I hoped that this was leading to your bed."

A moan escaped his lips. "Thank God you said that. I'm not sure there is a shower cold enough to cool me down."

Elliot continued to unbutton his shirt. "Then as an adult, I should tell you that I'm on birth control. I have an IUD, and I have a, shall we say, clean history."

"As do I, however…" his cheeks tinged pink, "I also have protection."

Elliot raised her eyebrows. "Do you always have condoms with you when you travel?"

He rubbed the back of his neck. "Not always, but this time I do."

She stopped unbuttoning. "And what's so special about this time?"

His ears burned red as he studied the floor. "Because my mum packed my bag."

Elliot threw back her head and laughed. "Your mother packed your bag, and she packed condoms?"

Albert cocked his head to the side. "I've never heard you laugh like that."

Elliot covered her mouth in horror. She'd allowed the Maleficent on cackle to rear its ugly head.

Al ran his fingers along the hollow of her throat. "That has to be the most infectious, authentic laugh I've ever heard."

"My mom said I sounded like a villain," she said sheepishly.

"I think it sounds sexy. It's raw, authentic."

She touched his bare chest. "You keep using the word 'authentic.' As if it were something special."

"It is special." He put his hands over hers. "You don't understand how rare it is to find somebody who appreciates me as just a plain old chap. When you look at me, you don't see an actor; you don't see the roles I play. You see me and not some cover boy."

"I wouldn't be so sure about that." She kissed the ticklish spot just below his earlobe. "When I look at you, I definitely see the sexiest man alive."

~ ~ ~

The next morning, a raucous knock awoke the lovers. "What the bloody hell?" Alfred groaned.

Elliot untangled herself from his arms, made her way to the door, and looked through the peephole. A woman in scrubs and a man in a business suit were standing in the hallway. Both were wearing surgical masks.

The man knocked again. "Mr. Moffat, Miss McCoy, we need to speak to you." His business-like tone set Elliot's teeth on edge.

"Just give us a second," she called as she raced to find something to wear.

When they finally opened the door, the woman handed two masks to Alfred. "Would you mind wearing these, please?"

Al kept his gaze on the woman as he handed Elliot her mask. "Can I ask what this is about?"

The man in the suit clasped his hands behind his back. "I'm Brian Lincoln, Vice President of Customer Service for Heathrow Air. You'll forgive me if I forego the handshake."

Elliot adjusted her mask. "Is this about the flight?"

Brian nodded. "As you know, one of our flight attendants tested positive for COVID-19."

Alfred furrowed his brow. "Isn't that why we are here, in quarantine?"

The woman in scrubs nodded. "I'm Dr. Alexandra Carr. A few people from the flight have begun to show symptoms."

Elliot grabbed Alfred's hand. "How many?"

Brian said, "We cannot disclose that information."

Alfred stood up straight. "Then why do we know the number of cases on those cruise ships?"

Dr. Carr quieted him with a stern look. "We're trying to keep the numbers quiet because people are on edge. The last thing we need is mass hysteria."

Elliot could see a genuine tiredness behind her stern demeanor. She put a hand on Al's shoulder. The gesture seemed to calm him.

The doctor continued, "We're offering tests to all passengers. This is voluntary; you are under no obligation to consent. The test results will be available in three days."

"What happens if we test positive?" Elliot asked.

"If you remain asymptomatic or your symptoms are mild, you'll be isolated. If your symptoms progress, you'll receive treatment at a local hospital."

"And if I choose not to test?" Alfred asked.

"If you remain symptom free, at the end of the fourteen-day quarantine, you can go along your merry way."

Elliot pinched the bridge of her nose. "Just so I understand, if we test negative, nothing changes. If we test positive, we get isolated, but not treated unless we show symptoms. If we do nothing and show symptoms, you will test us then?"

The doctor nodded affirmatively.

Alfred said, "The news says that there is a shortage of tests. Is that true?"

The doctor lowered her eyes. "I will not comment on that."

Elliot glanced at Alfred, and when their eyes met, she knew they agreed. She looked back to the doctor. "I'll take my chances. No test."

Dr. Carr sighed. "Would you consent to having your temperature taken twice a day?"

Alfred shrugged. "I have no issue with that."

"Me either," Elliot agreed.

Brian straightened his tie. "If you change your mind, or begin showing symptoms, please call the front desk right away."

Over the next few days, neither showed any symptoms of the COVID-19 virus, but just to be safe, they spent plenty of time in bed.

~ ~ ~

On the morning of their thirteenth day, they finished *Avengers: End Game*. During Iron Man's memorial, Elliot dabbed at her eyes. "I can't believe it's over." However, she was talking about so much more than the movie franchise. Their time was ending, her fairy tale dream with the British hunk would soon be replaced with the harsh reality of a world entrenched in a pandemic. Though she ached for those affected by the illness, her own selfish heart could only focus on one thing: he was leaving.

The heaviness of it all seemed to weigh upon Alfred as well. His usual boyish smile hardly ever graced his lips, and his body seemed heavy when he moved.

Over an unusually subdued dinner, Elliot asked, "So, what is your plan for tomorrow?"

"I came to the States to do reshoots around DC, but those have obviously been cancelled. I guess the only thing for me to do is go back home and social distance."

"Can you get a flight?"

"My agent chartered a plane to take me to London. It leaves tomorrow morning."

Elliot was not prepared for how much hearing the words would make her chest ache. She lowered her eyes. "That sounds very nice."

"What are your plans?"

"I'll head back to my townhouse. I only live about forty-five minutes from here, so my trip will be a lot shorter than yours." She tried to keep her voice light.

"It'll be good to be home, or at least to not be in a hotel room."

Elliot swallowed hard. "It is getting a bit claustrophobic, isn't it?" She reached for her glass of wine but sat it down when she saw that her hand was shaking. "What's the first thing you are going to do when you get to London?" She was desperate to get the topic off their looming separation.

"Usually, the first thing I would do is to meet with my manager, but people aren't meeting face to face." He shrugged. "So, probably, I would set up some Zoom meetings, rearrange my schedule. It's going to be suffocating."

Elliot refused to look at him, look into those green eyes. "I don't envy you."

His voice grew thick. "It'll also be exceptionally lonely."

The pain in his voice made her chest hurt. Without thinking, she reached for his hand and raised her eyes to meet his. He entwined his fingers with hers. "I don't want to be lonely."

Tears threatened to spill from her eyes. "I don't want to be lonely either."

"Then come with me."

Her throat constricted. "To England?" she managed to croak.

"Yes." Alfred took her hands in his. "Neither of us has anywhere we have to be."

Part of her wanted to hop on a private jet and throw caution to the wind, but Elliot was an adult. Her architecture firm was still trying to figure out how they were going to handle the looming shut down. And what if her mother or sister got sick? What would happen if she got to England, and he realized how broken she truly was but the airlines had shut down and she couldn't get home.

"I can't." She lowered her eyes.

"Why?"

"I just can't."

Albert motioned around the room. "What we have, what we've cultivated here within these four walls. I'm not ready to walk away without knowing what this can become."

"What if out there," she pointed to the window, "in the real world, what we have here doesn't translate to day-to-day life?"

He shrugged. "There is a chance that this oddball love affair, thrown together amid a global pandemic, isn't made for everyday life."

That was not the answer she wanted. Just once she wanted a man to fight for her, to convince her she was worth it. She closed her eyes to keep the tears from falling. Then she felt his knuckles running along her cheekbone.

She opened her eyes to see Alfred's eyes were also full of tears. "But I can tell you one thing, I don't' want to walk away without trying. I have been more authentic with you than most of my closest mates. You make me feel like an ordinary man, but in an exquisitely extraordinary way. I don't know what I can say, other than… please."

It broke her heart to say, "I can't go to London with you. Right now, things with my firm are tenuous. There are rumors of layoffs. I have to be ready to return to the office if I am needed."

Alfred shrugged. "Okay, then I'll come with you."

Her spine straightened. "Wait… What?"

"I said I'll come with you."

She looked at him through narrowed eyes. "You'd really give up the comforts of a London mansion to stay with me in an eighteen hundred square foot townhouse in West Virginia?"

He looked around the hotel room, the four walls that had witnessed them evolve from strangers to friends, then to lovers. The corners of his mouth turned up. "Do you have more than one bathroom?"

"Yes." Elliot laughed.

"Then a townhouse in West Virginia it is."

5

An Afternoon with Clara

October 11, 2012

Ally kept her head down and her shoulders slumped as she weaved between co-eds rushing to class. She wished she could disappear, but at five foot nine and two hundred pounds, it was difficult to go unnoticed. Resigned to the fact that she couldn't make herself disappear to the world, she pulled on her beanie, popped in her earbuds, and tried to make the world disappear to her. She set Pandora to the girl power station and marched forward as Pink instructed her how to *Raise Your Glass*.

She was lost in the gritty, vulnerable lyrics when Ally felt something smash into her chest. She took a step back, ready to release a semester's worth of pent-up ire on the co-ed. However, instead of a nose-in-their-phone frat boy, she saw a purple felt hat teetering atop a head of tight gray curls.

Without thinking, she reached out and grabbed the shoulders of the woman who had bumped into her. The woman's frame was sharp and angular under her green woolen coat. "Oh, excuse me," she said. Her voice was as brittle as the bones Ally could feel under her fingertips.

Ally held onto the elderly woman until she was sure she wouldn't topple over. "It's fine." She fought to keep the annoyance out of her voice.

"This wind really is something, isn't it?"

"It sure is," Ally said as she sidestepped the woman and the useless small talk.

"Do you attend school here?" the woman asked.

Ally's upbringing dictated that she shows her elders respect, even if she just wanted to be left along. So, she plastered a polite smile on her face and replied, "I do."

The woman looked around as if searching for something. "I don't want to be a bother, but..." she put her hand to her lips, "I'm looking for a particular place."

Ally silently cursed her respectful upbringing as she offered, "What place is it?"

"This city has changed so much; I hardly recognize anything." Her eyes scanned the pedestrian mall around them. "I went to college here decades ago, and there used to be a military base close by. Many of the enlisted men lived in this part of the town. Would you happen to know anything about that?"

Ally shrugged. "My roommate's dad told me that there used to be an Army base a few miles outside of town, but in the nineties, the D.O.D. closed it."

The older woman nodded. "My son told me that the base got shut down." She pulled a crumpled sheet of paper from her pocket. "But I saw on Google that Baker Street is close to here. There's a building there that holds a lot of memories for me, and I would like to visit one last time. Would you mind pointing me in the right direction?"

At the word "memories," the woman's crooked back straightened and a wistfulness clouded her eyes.

For years to come, Ally would look back on this moment and question why the old woman's expression had such an effect on her. Maybe it was because the frail woman evoked a deeply engrained compassion; maybe it was because she hoped to retain the type of spunk when she became elderly; or maybe it was because Ally desperately needed a distraction from her own thoughts. Whatever it was, that moment would stay with her for the rest of her life.

Ally took the woman's bony hand in hers. The blue vessels under her skin gave it a ghostly hue, a stark contrast to Ally's mocha complexion. "Baker Street is only two blocks from here. Would you like me to take you?"

The thin skin around the woman's eyes crinkled like crepe-paper when she smiled. "That would be just lovely. And by the way, call me Clara."

"Hello, Clara. I'm Ally."

~ ~ ~

Ally assumed the walk would take quite a while and prepared to reduce her quick stride, but Clara wasn't as frail as she seemed. The older woman had a spunk inside her that kept her step-in-step with the college girl, and within five minutes, the pair was standing in front of a brownstone apartment building.

Clara's gaze covered the building, as if she was trying to memorize each brick. As her eyes took in the scene, tears gathered on her lower lashes. She put her hand to her chest. "This is the place," she whispered.

"It's been a while since you've been here?" Ally asked as she took in the building. From the broken cement stairs and cracking mortar between the bricks, it looked like it had been a while since ANYBODY had been there.

Clara wiped away the tears that were leaving tracks on her powdered cheeks. "Yes. In a past life."

"Did you live here when you were in college?"

Clara ignored the question. "These memories are weighing heavily upon this old heart. Would you mind if we found a place to sit down?"

"There's a small park one block over. It's not a far walk. Would that be close enough?

Clara smiled and allowed Ally to lead her to the park and to a bench under a barren oak tree. They sat in silence for a few minutes and watched the gray squirrels flit about. Just as Ally was going to ask if she was okay, Clara said, "Thank you for bringing me, my dear. I didn't expect you to make the trip with me. You've been very kind."

"It's not a big deal." Ally gave a one-shoulder shrug. "I was looking for an excuse to get off campus today."

Clara pointed a bony finger in her direction. "Kindness is always a big deal."

"I guess it is."

"Can I ask you a personal question, dear?"

Ally studied the older woman with suspicion but figured the rest of the afternoon had been completely unscripted, so why listen to reason now. "Sure."

An Afternoon with Clara

Clara put her hand on Ally's knee. "What's making you so sad?"

Ally pulled away. "I'm sorry. What?"

"I didn't mean to pry." Clara pulled her hands back into her owl lap. "It's just that your eyes are clouded, and your shoulders slump as if they have the weight of the world upon them."

"You noticed that from just spending a few minutes with me?" This took Ally completely by surprise. She usually did such a good job of hiding her emotions; her dad had affectionately teased her with the nickname "Data," the name of the android from *Star Trek*. Not one single person in her work, in any of her classes, or even her roommate had picked up on the fact that she was falling apart inside. But this woman, this frail stranger, had seen through her mask.

Ally wanted to scoff, deny the charge, but before she could stop herself, she asked, "How can you tell?"

"Old woman's intuition." Clara tapped her temple.

Ally looked at the overcast sky and let out a wry laugh. "It's a stupid, boy problem. My nana tells me it's the type of thing that ten years from now will seem insignificant and trite."

"But it's significant now."

"Yeah, it is." Ally exhaled.

"Do you want to tell me about it?" Clara asked.

And though Ally didn't understand why, she DID want to tell Clara not just about her boy problems, but about everything that was bothering her. She wanted to open her mouth and lay all her cares at the woman's orthotic sneakers. "There are these two guys."

Clara raised a gray eyebrow. "And you have to decide between them?"

"How did you know?"

A mischievous grin tickled her lips. "I haven't always been an old woman."

Ally felt a smile spread across her face.

"Tell me, what are their names? What are they like?"

Ally fiddled with the pendant around her neck. "Well, there is Micah. He's an accounting major and was raised by his grandparents after his parents were killed in a car accident. He's rock-steady, dependable, all the things a woman wants."

"Did he give you that necklace?"

Ally looked down at the silver willow tree pendant and nodded. "He said that true love grows slowly like a tree; it establishes strong roots and is able to bend in the wind."

Clara nodded. "He sounds like he's wise beyond his years."

"He is. I tell him he's the oldest twenty-two-year-old I've ever met." She smiled warmly. "He's truly a remarkable person."

"So, what about this other young man?"

"Ben?" Ally exhaled heavily. "He's as different from Micah as can be. He's a bartender with no real plan for his future. He spends his weekends working on his Harley, rock-climbing, or paddle-boarding."

"He sounds exciting."

The warm smile vanished from Ally's lips, and an intense sparkle shone in her eyes. "Exciting, dangerous, unpredictable."

"Passionate?"

Ally's head snapped around, and her jaw dropped open.

A puckish spread across Clara's face. "Remember, I haven't always been this old."

"Yes, passionate." Ally laughed. "Sometimes I wish I could combine them; take my favorite parts of each and blend into the perfect man."

Clara grimaced. "That sounds a bit too much like Mary Shelley to me."

Ally threw back her head and laughed.

"What's so funny?" Clara asked.

"My dad calls me Dr. Frankenstein." Ally smiled. "I just got accepted to medical school. I start in the fall."

Clara clapped her hands in delight. "Well, congratulations! In my day, women were relegated to homemaker, nurse, or teachers. Your generation has so many more choices than I had." There was a longing in her voice. "Even the conundrum you face now, not many young women in my time had the option of choice. At a certain age, respectable young women were to settle down with the first principled gentleman to show her favor and begin a family."

"Is that what you did?"

Clara gave her a playful side eye. "No, much to my mother's chagrin."

Ally scooted closer. "What did you do?"

"I started nursing school when I was seventeen, which was completely acceptable. Then, at nineteen, I broke my mother's heart when I joined the Army Nurse Corp and went to Vietnam. I served as a charge nurse for a mobile unit for five years."

Ally shook her head in disbelief. This fragile woman had patched up wounded soldiers in a foreign jungle decades before she was born. She glanced at Clara, and for the briefest moment, she caught a steely glint in those ancient gray eyes. Ally could picture her, nineteen years old, five foot nothing, jaw set in determination as she faced unimaginable fear in a mobile ER. "I'm sure you have amazing stories."

Clara nodded. "I've held the legs of a forty-year-old woman while she pushed life into the world. More times than I wish to remember, I held the hand of an eighteen-year-old boy as he took his last breath." Her eyes darted abruptly to Ally. "Why do you want to be a doctor?"

Ally's back stiffened. The attention being placed on her took her off guard. "I've been a science junky since I can remember. I've always been fascinated by the human body, the intricacies of neurons, the mechanics of the joints. I know it sounds gross, but when I would find dead animals on the side of the road, if they didn't stink too bad, I'd take them home and dissect them. I needed to know how their bodies worked on the inside." She smiled. "My mom said I'd either grow up to be a doctor or a serial killer."

"Well, I'm glad you made the right decision." Clara covered her mouth and laughed. "My, how things have changed. In my day, a woman would never be allowed to be a doctor. Heck, when I returned from Vietnam, I was barely allowed to be a nurse." The far-off look returned to her eyes. "Over there, when there would be an influx of wounded, we'd go into triage mode. The surgeons took the direst cases. Nurses performed minor surgeries on their own, removing shrapnel, even amputations. We made life-or-death decisions. Sometimes it was up to us to decide who got treatment and lived, and who would receive morphine so that they could pass in peace. We called them the expectants." A shudder went through her frail body.

"I'm sure you were happy when you were able to come home and practice in America."

Clara made a sound like the air being let out of a tire. "Pshh, practice in America, my ass."

Ally was taken aback by the woman swearing.

"When I returned to nursing in the States, I wasn't even allowed to give an Aspirin without the approval of a doctor. I went from performing amputations to not being trusted to insert an I.V."

"That must have been so demeaning."

"Demeaning, demoralizing, insulting." The corners of her lips turned down. "It was still better than being called baby killer or commie slut."

Ally's heartbeat increased in outrage. How could anybody call this lovely human being such awful names? Clara was a soldier, a warrior, a woman who had laid the groundwork so that women like her could pursue whatever career they chose. She wanted to hug her tight, say "thank you," tell her how much she admired her, but all she could do was whisper, "You didn't deserve that."

Clara's steel gray eyes bore into hers. "I'm sure there are plenty of things you have faced that you didn't deserve either." She patted Ally's hand. "At least I was given the opportunity to be in a hospital when I returned home. Nurses of your complexion were only allowed to work in the cafeteria or laundry room. Such a waste of intelligence and talent." There wasn't pity in Clara's voice, just undeniable anger.

Ally took her hand. "Clara, I'm so happy that I met you!"

"The feeling is mutual, dear."

"If you didn't go back to nursing, what did you do?"

"I lived with my parents for a few months and worked at the local pharmacy." Her cheeks wrinkled as she smiled. "That's where I met Frank. He was a lovely man, a devoted father, an exemplary husband. We raised three amazing sons. I'm a great-grandmother now. Would you like to see a picture?"

Though Ally was not a "kid person," she felt obliged to nod. Clara fumbled in her purse for a moment, then pulled out a photo with well-worn edges. "His name is George. Isn't he just the cutest?"

Ally admired the image of a chubby-cheeked little boy. "He certainly is adorable." She handed the photo back to Clara. "So, you ended up going the wife-and-mother route?"

Clara nodded. "It fit me. Frank was a good man, and we had a beautiful life. I lost him last summer."

"I'm so sorry."

"Don't be. We had fifty-one amazing years." She smiled wistfully. "He was my best friend, and he helped heal the wounds that Vietnam created. He nursed me through breast cancer." She patted Ally's hand. "To be honest, he sounds a lot like your Micah."

Ally lowered her gaze. "So, you never had a Ben in your life."

"I wouldn't say that." Clara winked. "Frank was the love of my life, but he wasn't my first love. Didn't you wonder why an old woman would travel just to see an apartment complex?"

"I guess I never thought about it."

"That brick building we looked at," she pointed a bony finger toward the brown building, "will be demolished in a couple of days."

Ally took a closer look. Though she had noticed the crumbling steps and mortar, she hadn't noticed the yellow tape blocking the entry way or the fact that none of the windows had blinds. "Did you live there when you were in college?" she asked.

"No, that's where Tommy lived."

Ally's eyes grew wide. "Tommy?"

Pink-tinged Clara's cheeks. "Tommy was, well… Tommy was special. Just after I got out of nursing training, we met at a USO dance. He was charming, and he could dance like an angel." Clara covered her heart with her hand. "And he was handsome. He had the loveliest blue eyes you've ever seen."

The picture was becoming clear. "So, Tommy was before Frank?"

Clara nodded. "I loved them both, but in very different ways. Much like how you love Micah and Ben."

Ally toyed with one of her braids. "I don't know if I even know what love is. I mean, if I truly loved either one of them, then no other man would matter. Right? He would be all I could think about?"

Clara let out a small giggle. "Oh sweetie, you've been watching the Hallmark channel too long. Love isn't something that can be placed in a neat little box and tied with a velvet bow." She shook her head. "Love is messy; it guts you, tears you open, and leaves you exposed and vulnerable. Sometimes you are on top of the world, and sometimes, you're a puddle at the bottom of a ravine."

Clara closed her eyes, then turned her face and allowed the October sunlight to warm her cheeks. The soft light highlighted every wrinkle and every age spot. In that moment, Ally thought Clara was the most beautiful woman she had ever laid eyes upon. Each line around her eyes and dark spot upon her cheek were stripes she had earned. Each highlighted, not her age, but her experience and wisdom. When she opened her eyes again, there were tears clinging to her lower lashes. She caught her breath as she inhaled. "Tommy was killed in Vietnam."

"Oh!" Ally exhaled. The revelation that Clara's first love had died in Vietnam was a tragic link that brought the past into the present. "I'm so sorry."

"Thank you." Clara patted her knee.

A thought cut Ally to her core. Was Tommy one of the young men Clara had helped pass into the next life? Had she watched the man she loved die? Ally swallowed hard. "Did Tommy…" she started to ask.

Clara shook her head as if she knew the question. "Tommy was shot down over Dak To; thankfully, I was nowhere near there."

"Oh," was all Ally could say.

Clara continued, "When Tommy and I met at a USO dance, I didn't know my orders, but he knew he was being sent to Vietnam in two weeks. We get so complacent today, thinking that tomorrow is a guarantee. When you're twenty-three and know you are being sent into a war zone, you look at life differently."

Ally couldn't find her voice, so she nodded.

"After that dance, we snuck off base to a little diner. He ordered one milkshake with two straws. When we were finished, we came to this very park, and we danced under the stars. There was no music, so he sang to me: The Everly Brothers, Dean Martin, and Patsy Cline. He could sing as gracefully as he danced." She wiped away a tear sliding down her cheek. "It probably sounds cliché and silly to kids today."

"It sounds amazing."

Clara smiled. "We spent the week together, every second that we were free. He was my first love; he was my first a lot of things." Pink tinged her cheeks.

Ally put her hand to her mouth. "I'm sure that was scandalous."

"You have no idea." The lines crinkled around her eyes as she smiled. "But we loved one another so fiercely. If he'd have asked me to marry him, I would have done it in a heartbeat. Love like that, passionate and all-consuming, doesn't come around very often."

"But he didn't ask."

Clara shook her head. "We were both heading off into a war zone, same war, different zones."

"If he had come home, do you think you would have married?" Ally asked.

"Perhaps." She sighed. "The thing is, if we had married, I don't know if it would have lasted. There's a reason passion like that only happens once in a lifetime; it burns white-hot, but it burns fast. I don't know if men like Tommy could settle down and make good husbands or fathers. When I got the letter telling me he had been shot down over Dak To, I never thought my heart could be put back together."

"I can't imagine?"

Clara's lips turned up on the corners. "But then I came home, and I met Frank. You know the rest."

Ally lowered her eyes. "Do you think I should choose Micah over Ben?"

"To be fair, I don't think I have the right to have any opinion about it. All I know is my story, and in my story, Tommy was a lyrical poem, while Frank was my novel. You get to be the author of your story."

"Why did you want to see Tommy's building one last time?"

"Because it was a chapter I wished to revisit. That is all."

Ally shifted on the bench. She had been so engrossed in Clara's story; she didn't realize how cold it had gotten. The sun was now setting behind the mountains and a chill was enveloping her. She flexed her fingers trying to get circulation moving, and realized if she was feeling the biting cold, Clara was probably faring worse.

"Would you like to get a coffee or perhaps hot chocolate? There is a Black Dog Café on the pedestrian mall where we met."

Clara rubbed her hands together as if just noticing the chill. "I would like that, but there's something I would like to do first, if you would help me."

"What is it?"

"I know it would be trespassing, but I would like to walk through Tommy's old apartment one more time. I don't know why, but I feel drawn to it, like a story that I never got to finish."

Ally looked at the brownstone building and then back to Clara. "Okay, but we have to be fast."

Hand in hand, they walked toward the building. Ally held up the yellow tape across the entryway, then followed Clara inside. The air smelled of mold and sawdust, and the floorboards creaked under their feet as they walked down the hallway. Two-thirds of the way down, Clara stopped and turned toward a doorway. "221 B, this is the one."

She pushed on the door, and with a small whine of protest, it swung open. They walked into the apartment, and though Ally saw only empty rooms, from the look in Clara's eyes, she could tell the older woman was seeing a completely different vision.

Clara walked to the kitchen and touched the dripping faucet. "This is where I made his breakfast." She stood in the middle of the living room. "This is where we danced to Patsy Cline." She walked to the single bedroom and held her hand to her heart. "This is where we..." she trailed off.

Clara stopped in each corner, addressing each memory, each experience, each ghost. When she was finished, she walked to the doorway and ran her fingers along the door jamb. "This is where we shared our last kiss. He didn't want me coming to the send-off. He said that he couldn't let his men see him break down." A tear slipped from the corner of her eye. She wiped it away and then looked to Ally. "Would you walk me back now? I'm ready to go."

Without a word, Ally took her hand and led Clara onto the front stoop. The sun was now almost fully set, casting an orange glow over the street.

As they walked toward the coffee shop, Ally spotted a woman walking toward them. She was wearing blue jeans, a red parka, and hiking boots. Her gold-silver hair stuck out from under an *Iron Ivy* hat, and Ally guessed her to be in her mid-sixties. The woman's pace quickened as she approached the building.

"Hello, I'm sorry to intrude, but is this Baker Street?"

Clara and Ally both nodded. The woman smiled. "Do you know if this is the building that used to be apartments for servicemen in the fifties?"

Clara and Ally exchange confused looks, then Clara answered, "It is."

The stranger looked at the yellow caution tape hanging in the main doorway. "And it's getting ready for demolition?"

Ally nodded.

The stranger said, "My parents lived here for a short period of time. It is where I was born. I know it may sound strange, but I wanted to see this piece of my history before it's gone."

Clara chuckled. "Not strange at all."

The woman leaned against the railing. "Right before my dad shipped to Vietnam, my mom and I returned to West Virginia. I was too young to remember." She chewed her bottom lip. "He died during the war. All I have of him are pictures."

"I'm so sorry," Ally said.

"Thank you." She stared at the building. "I know it sounds silly, but I was thinking if I could stand in the room where he stood, I might be able to connect with him." The woman pulled a scrap of paper from her pocket. "I know it is a long shot, but do you know which apartment is 221B?"

Clara studied the stranger, her hand raised to her mouth. "Has anybody ever told you that you have the loveliest blue eyes?" she said.

The woman smiled. "Thank you. Everybody says I have my father's eyes."

Ally was afraid the shock would topple Clara on the spot; she put her arm around the older woman, but it wasn't needed. Clara stood steady as a statue. And though she couldn't hide the expression of pain on her face, Clara held her head high with dignity as she pointed to the yellow caution tape. "I believe I saw 221 B down this hallway on the left."

The woman's eyes sparkled. "Thank you so much! You've been a Godsend!"

The walk back to the pedestrian mall was quieter and colder than the walk to Baker Street. Ally had so many questions, but Clara seemed lost in her memories, and Ally didn't want to intrude.

Once they were seated by the fireplace at The Black Dog Café, Ally broke the silence. She sat her mug on the table and took Clara's hand. "I'm so sorry."

Clara squeezed back. "Don't be sorry. I'm not."

"You're not?" Ally couldn't hide the shock in her voice.

Clara made a dismissive motion with her hand. "I don't believe in regrets, but part of me has always wondered what might have been. Now, I know."

Ally leaned her forearms on the table. "Why didn't you tell her the truth?"

"Why would I besmirch the memory of her father? She obviously admired him, knowing that in his last month on Earth he'd made a mistake? Nah. Tommy exuded bravado, but at night, when he thought I was asleep, I could hear him cry. He was terrified to go to battle. Maybe that is why he found comfort in the arms of a mistress."

"You were not his mistress!" Ally said a bit too loud. She looked around to see if anybody else had heard, then lowered her voice. "You didn't know he was married."

Clara shook her head. "He told me he'd gotten a 'Dear John' letter when he received his orders." She took a sip of coco.

"See, you are blameless."

"Blame is a pointless game we play to make ourselves feel better about our own transgressions." Clara sat her cup down with a clink. "What happened in that apartment is in the past, though. Nothing good would have come of me telling my story today."

"I disagree."

Clara raised her eyebrows.

"Maybe it wouldn't have been helpful to that woman, but your story has been wonderful for me to hear. Your wisdom, your experiences, the good and bad have taught me so much." To Ally's surprise, she was on the verge of tears, and she was not a crier. In fact, she hadn't cried since her dog died when she was twelve.

Clara gave a playful wink. "Well, then I'm happy I made the trip."

"Me too." Ally smiled. "Where will you go now?"

Clara shrugged. "I have a bus ticket to take me to my grandson's home in Delancy."

"That's only a half-hour drive; I can take you."

"I don't want to put you out."

"Clara, I want to soak up every ounce of your wisdom while I have the chance."

April 8, 2017

Ally lay back against the pillows, more exhausted than she had ever been in her entire life. Even with the epidural, the twenty-two-hour labor had been grueling.

"Just one more push," the doctor urged. "I can see the top of his head."

Micah took her hand in his. The absence of his wedding band felt strange to her. One of the junior accountants at his firm had told Micah a horror story about a woman who had squeezed her husband's hand so tight during delivery that she'd bent his ring and had to have it cut off. Men were so emotional.

He brought her fingers to his lips and kissed. "You got this, babe. Just one more."

Ally nodded weakly, grabbed her thighs, and pushed herself to the edge of her physical limitations.

"His head's out! His head's out." Micah was literally jumping up and down with excitement. "Honey, he has a head full of hair. He's so handsome!"

"How can you tell? He's face down?" she demanded.

"I can just tell. He's gorgeous." Micah beamed.

"One more push to get the body out," the doctor instructed.

Clara wanted to jerk her leg from the stirrup and kick the man at the end of the table square in the nose for sounding so chipper while she was literally on the brink of death. She didn't care that the attending OB, Jarod, was one of her best friends from Med School; she wanted his blood.

"Ally, just one more push. That's it. I promise," Jarod instructed. Ally gritted her teeth, grabbed her thighs, and pushed one last time. She felt a sudden gush, then she heard the most beautiful, high-pitched wail she'd ever heard.

No longer angry, exhausted, and elated, she started at the overhead lights. "When do I get to hold my son?"

The nurse looked at the newborn and then at the mother. "Well, ah."

Though her legs were still in the stirrups, Ally sat straight up. "What's wrong? I want to see my son!" she screamed. "Jarod, give me my son!"

A shocked smile spread across Micah's face. "Nothing is wrong. The baby is healthy, sweetheart."

"Then what is it?" She frantically searched all the faces in the delivery room for any clue.

Finally, a broad grin spread across the doctor's face. "I don't know when you will hold your son, but as soon as I cut the umbilical cord, you can hold your daughter."

Ally fell back against the mattress. "Daughter? But, but, but..." Ally stammered.

Micah gazed at the screaming bundle at the foot of the bed. Tears ran into his beard. "She's gorgeous, Ally; simply gorgeous."

When Jarod finally laid the infant upon Ally's chest, he laughed. "Remember, regardless of how many sonograms we did, the baby would not cooperate? Well, it looks like you have one strong-willed little girl to raise."

Ally looked down at the dark-haired angel lying on her chest, and she felt a feeling of love envelop her like she had never known.

The baby had sweet little eyes, and her skinny little fingers were balled into a fist. Ally touched her perfect cheek.

"She's amazing," she whispered.

"She's beautiful like her mother." Micah wiped his cheeks. "But what are we going to name her? She doesn't look like an Owen."

Ally gently kissed her daughter, then looked to her husband. "I've always liked the name 'Clara.'"

About the Author

L aurel was born and raised in the beautiful mountains of West Virginia. She graduated with a Bachelor of Science in Mathematics and a Bachelor of Arts in Education from Fairmont State College (now Fairmont University). She earned a Master of Education from West Virginia University.

She married her best friend, Brian, in 2003. They have two wonderful daughters and continue to live in The Mountain State. When she is not writing or working her day job as a high school math teacher, she loves spending time with her wonderful husband and two brilliant daughters. They share their home with three sassy pound kitties and a loyal rescue mutt.

To reach Laurel

Author website:

www.laurelkile.com

Facebook:

www.facebook.com/laurelkileauthor

Instagram:

www.instagram.com/laurelkileauthor

TikTok:

www.tiktok/laurelkileauthor

Random Thoughts from the Author

As I was waiting for this collection to be formatted, the world lost one of its most talented storytellers, Jimmy Buffett. Jimmy's songs could easily be the soundtrack of my life. Leaving my family's farm to go to a large university: *The City*. Transitioning from college kid to working adult: *Changes in Latitudes, Changes in Attitudes*. Taking a celebratory trip to Key West after I finished my master's degree: *Tin Cup Chalice*. Rocking my baby girl to sleep: *Little Miss Magic*. I could go on and on.

Jimmy Buffett wasn't political. He never wrote a song that will be chanted by protesters. He never appeared on Capitol Hill. However, without a doubt, he changed the world. He gave people a place to find shelter from the storm, he brought people from all walks of life together, and above all, he made people happy.

Jimmy Buffett was living proof that our stories, no matter how whimsical or far-fetched, have power.

I hope you have enjoyed the stories I have crafted. Though I will never claim to be in the same category as Jimmy, I hope that they have provided a bit of respite from whatever storm you may be facing.

Fins up,

Laurel

PS. If you liked my stories, please consider leaving a positive review on Amazon, Goodreads, or any other platform.

Acknowledgements

To Ty Keenum and Sandy Springs Press, thank you for your wisdom and guidance. I will forever be grateful for your patience with a newbie.

To my sensitivity reader, Niece McCoy. Your insight and kindness made this possible.

To my mom. There are no words to express my gratitude for everything you have done for me. You and Dad always believed in my writing. I wish he could be here to see it.

To my husband, Brian. You are my partner, my soulmate, my unwilling beta reader and my most fierce cheerleader. Thank you for the nights you were an only dad so I could meet a deadline.

To my daughters, you inspire me every day. Never stop dreaming.

To each and every one of you who has read, beta read, advised, listened, reviewed, or just simply sent me love, THANK YOU a million times over.

Other Titles by the Author

Allegheny Front

Sometimes a lie reveals a larger truth.

After a grueling school year, Kate escapes to Pocahontas County, West Virginia to rest and rejuvenate. Unfortunately, a hundred-year flood hits and turns her vacation into an emergency evacuation. After relocating to a mountaintop resort, she finds an unconscious man in the woods, a man whose face she would recognize anywhere. Her celebrity crush, Jeremy Fulton.

When Jeremy regains consciousness, he introduces himself as Tim Jones and confides that he came into the wilderness to escape his hectic life. As they grow closer, Kate deals with the conundrum: can she let him know how she feels without telling him she knows his true identity?

When Tales Get Twisted

When Tales Get Twisted crazy things happen to our beloved classics.

When Catpunzel, a golden-haired kitten, is abandoned by her parents, a mysterious tabby named Gothel swoops in and adopts the child. Everything seems wonderful, but when Catpunzel befriends a boy named Tom, she sees a different side of Gothel—a side that will go to extraordinary lengths to keep her locked in her tower forever.

Redmoon Chase learns that her nana is ill and volunteers to bring her a basket of goodies. When Red arrives at her nana's house, she finds a big, bad real estate developer holding Nana hostage. Red must use her wits to save the cottage, her grandmother, and herself.

After being forced to move to Pennsylvania with her wicked stepmother, Whitney Snow finally escapes. She is befriended by a pack of seven, scraggly dogs who can speak human. Will Whitney's cunning, and the magical mutts' bravery be enough to thwart her stepmother's plot for revenge?

www.ingramcontent.com/pod-product-compliance
Lightning Source LLC
LaVergne TN
LVHW010210070526
838199LV00062B/4528